HS AC
HOMELAND SECUR
OPERATIONAL ANALYSIS CEN

An Assessment of the Joint Requirements Council's (JRC) Organization and Staffing

MICHAEL VASSEUR, DWAYNE M. BUTLER, BRANDON CROSBY,
BENJAMIN N. HARRIS, CHRISTOPHER SCOTT ADAMS

Published in 2018

Preface

As part of a larger ongoing study, the Homeland Security Operational Analysis Center (HSOAC) was asked to provide the Department of Homeland Security (DHS) Joint Requirements Council (JRC) with a quick-turn, three-month review of its business processes to recommend actions to improve its efficiency, effectiveness, and ability to plan for the future. The JRC is an executive-level body charged with building a unified, effective, and efficient operational requirements process for DHS as an enterprise. This review includes examination of best practices among similar organizations, interviews with JRC staff, and a JRC-specific analytic framework to examine four mission areas of the JRC: implementation and execution of the Joint Requirements Integration and Management System, provision of training to DHS staff on the requirements process, analysis of joint capabilities and requirements, and requirements outreach. Across mission areas, we find challenges in the organization and personnel systems of the JRC. The findings in this report should be of interest to JRC staff, DHS components, and DHS stakeholders impacted by the requirements review process.

This research was sponsored by the JRC and conducted within the Acquisition and Development Program of HSOAC federally funded research and development center (FFRDC).

About the Homeland Security Operational Analysis Center

The Homeland Security Act of 2002 (§ 305 of Public Law 107-296, as codified at 6 U.S.C. § 185), authorizes the Secretary of Homeland Security, acting through the Under Secretary for Science and Technology, to establish one or more FFRDCs to provide independent analysis of homeland security issues. The RAND Corporation operates the Homeland Security Operational Analysis Center as an FFRDC for DHS under contract HSHQDC-16-D-00007.

The HSOAC FFRDC provides the government with independent and objective analyses and advice in core areas important to the department in support of policy development, decisionmaking, alternative approaches, and new ideas on issues of significance. The HSOAC FFRDC also works with and supports other federal, state, local, tribal, and public- and private-sector organizations that make up the homeland security enterprise. The HSOAC FFRDC's research is undertaken by mutual consent with DHS and is organized as a set of discrete tasks. This report presents the results of research and analysis conducted under HSHQDC-17-J-00043, Joint Requirements Council Requirements Analysis Support.

The results presented in this report do not necessarily reflect official DHS opinion or policy.

For more information on HSOAC, see www.rand.org/hsoac.

For more information on this publication, visit www.rand.org/t/RR2473.

Contents

Boxes and Figures

Tables

Summary

The Joint Requirements Council (JRC) is an executive-level body in the Department of Homeland Security (DHS) charged with building a unified, effective, and efficient operational requirements process for DHS. The JRC's mission is to create a more effective, efficient organization within DHS via the establishment of an enterprise-wide, component-driven requirements process. The JRC is responsible for endorsing and prioritizing validated capability needs for enterprise-wide and component-specific capabilities across the 14 operational and support organizations that make up DHS.[1] Given that the JRC is a relatively new organization, JRC leadership tasked the Homeland Security Operational Analysis Center (HSOAC) with a quick-turn review of its business processes to offer actions to improve its efficacy and effectiveness and to improve its ability to plan for the future.

Methodology

Our assessment of JRC business processes adapts DHS's Doctrine, Organization, Training, Materiel, Leadership, Personnel, Facilities Plus Regulations, Grants, and Standards (DOTMLPF+R/G/S) framework to examine select JRC mission areas; identify challenges faced by these efforts; and recommend areas of focus for potential solutions or more detailed future analysis.[2] This assessment includes documentation of current business processes across the four primary mission areas that we determined

---

[1] Operational and support components that currently make up the DHS include U.S. Citizenship and Immigration Services; U.S. Customs and Border Protection; U.S. Coast Guard; Federal Emergency Management Agency; Federal Law Enforcement Training Center; U.S. Immigration and Customs Enforcement; Transportation Security Administration; U.S. Secret Service; Directorate for Management; National Protection and Programs Directorate; Science and Technology Directorate; Countering Weapons of Mass Destruction Office; Office of Intelligence and Analysis; and the Office of Operations Coordination.

[2] Our analysis began with a DOTMLPF+R/G/S framework, but we present only a subset of criteria in our results. Ultimately, we found no analytic gains from including Regulations, Grants, and Standards in our analysis. As such, the analysis presented in this report uses the standard DOTMLPF framework used by the military. See Chapter Two for additional details.

to be most critical to the success of the JRC, based on a review of authoritative JRC documents, the JRC mission, and discussions with JRC subject-matter experts. These areas represent the tasks the JRC is currently mandated to perform and are intended to capture the activities JRC staff routinely engage in as part of the DHS-wide requirements process. The four primary mission areas of focus are:

- **implementation and execution of the Joint Requirements Integration and Management System (JRIMS) process.** The JRIMS process is the primary function of the JRC and serves to review and validate component-level requirements. Components submit requirements documents for new capability gaps to the JRC for initial review, comments from across DHS, and ultimately a validation recommendation to the JRC principals (executive-level representatives from across DHS) who endorse and validate the documents.
- **provision of requirements training to DHS staff on the requirements process** through multiday workshops led by JRC staff.
- **analysis of joint capabilities and requirements**, including assessing capabilities across DHS to create a prioritized list of gaps for the department and assessing existing programs to provide input to senior leaders on investment and funding decisions.
- **requirements outreach to various enterprise-wide forums related to requirements**, as well as external engagements with entities outside of DHS.

We examined these processes using a multimethod approach. First, we developed a general understanding of the challenges facing the JRC today and defined each JRC mission area and framework element to guide later assessments. Second, we reviewed literature on best practices and common pitfalls among other joint requirements councils for their applicability to the JRC. Third, we reviewed literature relevant to organizations with complex missions, such as the JRC. We consider the JRC mission complex, as it works in a decentralized environment across the diverse range of DHS missions—DHS components are the primary drivers of requirements, without an analogue to the Department of Defense (DoD) Joint Staff to coordinate efforts (see U.S. Government Accountability Office, 2016). This review identified potential challenge areas for the JRC. Fourth, we interviewed JRC program staff to understand their roles, responsibilities, and the overall structure of the JRC office and assessed the challenges that arise as a result. Finally, we combined emerging insights across JRC mission areas through a JRC-specific adaptation of the DOTMLPF framework.[3] We conclude by offering immediate and longer-term recommendations.

---

[3] The DOTMLPF framework is a method to identify risks, challenges, and possible mechanisms to address these issues across materiel and nonmateriel solutions. We use it as an organizing principle to codify challenges in our assessment in an organized fashion.

Emergent Findings and Preliminary Recommendations

We assessed each DOTMLPF category and mission area combination based on the challenges identified in our assessment. Table S.1 presents our summary assessment of the category/mission area combinations, with more-detailed discussions available in the body of the report. Combinations are coded green if no challenges were noted during our assessment. Combinations coded amber are those that present a challenge that if addressed would provide positive benefits to JRC staff, but are not in need of immediate attention. Combinations coded red present immediate problems to JRC effectiveness and/or efficacy and should be addressed as soon as possible. We find that the JRC faces two major challenges: its organizational relationship to DHS components and its staffing levels.

Organization

The JRC faces significant challenges, based on the nature of its relationship to the DHS components. JRC mission areas are based on a "component-led and component-driven" requirements process, according to authoritative documentation and several interviews with JRC staff. As a result of the decentralized nature of requirements decisionmaking within DHS, JRC staff face considerable role uncertainty in their work. Many interview subjects expressed that the only certain aspect of their work was uncertainty. Literature links this type of uncertainty to a variety of negative outcomes, including lower employee well-being and satisfaction and decreased job performance (Griffin, Neal, and Parker, 2007; Cooper et al., 2015). Similar negative impacts are noted over the long term for organizations that are understaffed (Hudson and Shen, 2015; Ganster

Table S.1
Summary of JRC DOTMLPF Categories by Mission Area

Category	JRIMS	Requirements Training	Joint Analysis	Outreach
Doctrine				
Organization				
Training				
Materiel				
Leadership				
Personnel				
Facilities				

NOTE: Assessment based on interviews with JRC staff, and application of Joint Council best practices and organizational literature to the JRC. Details on specific challenges are available in the main body of the report. Green = No challenge noted during assessment; amber = minor issue: addressing would produce positive benefits for JRC staff; red = major issue: should be addressed immediately to ameliorate negative impacts on JRC efficiency and/or effectiveness.

and Rosen, 2013; Ton, 2008). This research suggests that significant uncertainty can be as debilitating for an organization's effectiveness as a lack of personnel.

While a certain amount of uncertainty is inherent in the decentralized way the JRC interacts with DHS components, measures should be taken to mitigate uncertainty's adverse effects. Increasing outreach efforts and vesting increased authority in the JRC over the requirements process would follow the best practices we identified among other joint requirements councils and could also improve JRC effectiveness and efficiency. Specifically, the JRC lacks any authority over existing programs or authority to tie budgets to validated requirements; it receives most of its information from the component sponsor of a requirement. A JRC with more robust authority over joint requirements, including over component actions, would improve its effectiveness, enhance its ability to take an enterprise-wide view of requirements, and reduce the task uncertainty imposed on staff.

To address challenges associated with uncertainty, **we recommend that DHS further analyze, and consider giving the JRC more authority over, DHS component requirements, including those for existing programs.** These additional authorities can be thought of as an initial step identified by our application of joint council best practice to the JRC and staff interviews. Specifying how best to execute these authorities, the required increase in outreach to the components, and the resulting relationship between the JRC and DHS components would require analysis of each component's requirements process that was beyond the scope of this effort. Such analyses could be conducted using the framework established in this report, which would streamline the process of comparing component and JRC processes.

Personnel

The JRC faces significant staffing challenges across all mission areas. We conclude that the JRC is understaffed, given the current breadth of its responsibilities. There is evidence that staffing has increased along with JRIMS demands, but not at a pace required to fully meet all demands on the JRC staff. JRC staffing increases, primarily in the analysis section, have been sufficient to keep pace with the increased volume of JRIMS documents submitted, but interview subjects indicated this has done little to help them address demands placed on their time in other mission areas. This tension is felt across mission areas: The JRC currently lacks a single full-time staff member dedicated to training, has limited analyst time for the analysis of joint capabilities and requirements, and requires the majority of its staff to balance the needs of keeping to the deadlines established in the JRIMS manual with their outreach responsibilities. Chapter Three discusses literature that suggests that understaffing can lead to a "pulling together effect," in which team members work harder to make up for their small numbers in the short run, but there are negative consequences for employee well-being, satisfaction, and ability to sustain high work quality in the long run.

To address this challenge, **we recommend that DHS further analyze and consider increasing JRC staffing above current staff and contractor support levels by seven additional full-time equivalent (FTE) positions to better reflect workload across all current JRC mission areas based on demands that have arisen in the JRC's implementation journey.**[4] Additional analysis staff would allow the JRC to more fully engage with complex documents and develop expertise with a component's requirements, while additional front-office staff would support other JRC efforts that enhance the effort to establish a broader requirement community within DHS. In Chapter Five, we offer a macro-level assessment of staffing increases and their distribution across mission areas but acknowledge that a precursor to implementing these and future increases in staffing will likely require manpower analysis to effectively determine the purposes for which additional staff could best be utilized.

---

[4] FTE is the method used for estimating budgeting positions in the civilian service of the U.S. government. Estimation is done by hours of work rather than by position. According to the Office of Management and Budget, "[FTE] employment means the total number of regular straight-time hours worked (i.e., not including overtime or holiday hours worked) by employees divided by the number of compensable hours applicable to each fiscal year" (U.S. Office of Management and Budget, 2015).

Acknowledgments

We thank the Department of Homeland Security Joint Requirements Council staff for providing us with guidance and data during this study. We would particularly like to thank all the Joint Requirements Council (JRC) staff members who agreed to be interviewed in support of this project. Specifically, we would like to thank JRC Director Vincent DeLaurentis and Director of Analysis Al Sweetser for their time and input on this study.

We also thank RAND Corporation colleagues who provided invaluable comments, inputs, and guidance to the study, specifically Isaac Porche and Emma Westerman. Philip S. Antón, Jeff Drezner, Maria Lytell, John Parmentola, Marek Posard, and Brendan Toland provided peer reviews and greatly improved earlier versions of this report.

Abbreviations

CEO	chief executive officer
CGA	Capability Gap Assessment
DoD	U.S. Department of Defense
DHS	U.S. Department of Homeland Security
DNI	Director of National Intelligence/Directorate of National Intelligence
DOTMLPF+R/G/S	Doctrine, Organization, Training, Materiel, Leadership, Personnel, Facilities Plus Regulations, Grants, and Standards
FFRDC	federally funded research and development center
FTE	full-time equivalent
FY	fiscal year
GAO	U.S. Government Accountability Office
HSOAC	Homeland Security Operational Analysis Center
IRPDA	Independent Review Panel for Defence Acquisition
IRTPA	Intelligence Reform and Terrorism Prevention Act
ISO	International Organization for Standardization
IT	information technology
JAR	Joint Assessment of Requirements
JCS	Joint Chiefs of Staff
JICC	Joint Intelligence Community Council

JRC	Joint Requirements Council
JRIMS	Joint Requirements Integration and Management System
JROC	Joint Requirements Oversight Council
JSOC	Joint Special Operations Command
PMO	Program Management Office
PMP	Project Management Professional
UK JROC	United Kingdom Joint Requirements Oversight Council
USCG	U.S. Coast Guard
USSOCOM	U.S. Special Operations Command

CHAPTER ONE

Introduction

The Joint Requirements Council (JRC) is an executive-level body in the U.S. Department of Homeland Security (DHS) charged with building a unified, effective, and efficient operational requirements process for DHS.[1] This requirements process is to be an enterprise-wide, component-driven requirements process. The JRC is responsible for endorsing and prioritizing validated capability needs for enterprise-wide and component-specific capability gaps (DHS, 2003).[2] The JRC was formed in June 2014 as part of the Unity of Effort initiative, and it first gained permanent staff in June 2015.

Since 2015, the staffing level and composition of the JRC have changed as the organization has developed and implemented the Joint Requirements Integration and Management System (JRIMS) manual (signed in April 2016). The JRIMS manual outlines the process by which DHS requirements are to be analyzed and validated by the JRC. The JRC is currently organized into two parts: (1) an analysis section and (2) a program management office (PMO) or "front-office" section, both of which report to the JRC director and chairman. The analysis section primarily reviews requirements documents through the JRIMS process and interfaces with DHS components, while the front office handles executive-level communication and preparation, conducts office operations and maintenance, and develops longer-term strategic initiatives for the JRC. In total, the JRC currently has 13 employees. The JRC analysis section has six employees, five analysts, and the director of analysis, as well as additional federally

---

[1] Although used similarly, *joint* in the DHS context has several important differences from *joint* as used in a Department of Defense (DoD) context. In military usage, joint refers to the need for forces from various services to fight together as part of a joint whole. In a DHS context, there is no assumption of common operation, but instead common standards and integration in requirements analysis across the components. DHS is not working to ensure that two components execute missions together, but rather to ensure that they are applying similar levels of rigor to requirements decisionmaking and are taking advantage of any possible cost savings through combined acquisitions. Throughout this report, when we discuss the JRC, we use the DHS definition of joint.

[2] These operational and support components currently make up DHS: U.S. Citizenship and Immigration Services; U.S. Customs and Border Protection; U.S. Coast Guard (USCG); Federal Emergency Management Agency; Federal Law Enforcement Training Center; U.S. Immigration and Customs Enforcement; Transportation Security Administration; U.S. Secret Service; Directorate for Management; National Protection and Programs Directorate; Science and Technology Directorate; Countering Weapons of Mass Destruction Office; Office of Intelligence and Analysis; and the Office of Operations Coordination.

funded research and development center (FFRDC) analyst contractor support. The front office section of the JRC has six employees, including administrative contractor support.

Challenges Facing the Joint Requirements Council

Like every organization, the JRC faces vulnerabilities and obstacles that can impede efficient operations. These challenges could affect the JRC's ability to carry out its mission, and a careful understanding of potential challenges is needed to help JRC leadership identify appropriate solutions to mitigate or eliminate these challenges. In this report, we focus on two primary categories of challenges: complexity and the JRC's relative newness as an organization.

Complexity

The JRC is a complex organization within DHS, which is an even more complex organization. An organization's complexity is related to the number of subcomponents within the organization, the number of functions the organization performs, and the complexity or difficulty of performing these functions and supporting processes (Sargut and McGrath, 2011). An organization's level of complexity is also related to the number of stakeholders (both within and outside the organization) who have a role in executing the organization's functions: The more stakeholders involved, the greater the need for integration and collaboration. The complexity of stakeholder collaborations can be exacerbated by the level or autonomy of stakeholder organizations.

These criteria for defining complexity apply to the JRC in many ways, including the following:

- There are 14 operational and support component organizations within DHS.
- These organizations are led by high-ranking political appointees and federal career civilians.
- The roles and missions of some of these organizations do not overlap much with those of the JRC, thereby making it more difficult to integrate missions across organizations and execute the corresponding requirements.
- Conversely, some components have roles and missions very similar to those of the JRC, thus requiring deliberate efforts to avoid redundancy and streamline requirements.
- Interdependence across the organizations results in a need for synchronization.
- The wide range of requirements processes used by different organizations increases the challenge.

Complexity within the JRC is to a great extent the function of the complexity and diversity of DHS's varied missions, which include the executive protection mission of the U.S. Secret Service, the Transportation Security Administration's mission of securing the nation's transportation system, the Domestic Nuclear Detection Office mission of preventing nuclear terrorism, and USCG's 11 maritime missions, including search and rescue. Each of these missions is complex in its own right and has its own unique requirements. The diversity of DHS missions means that the JRC must be able to address a range of mission activities in its analysis of capabilities and joint requirements.

This complexity is further magnified by the decentralized nature of DHS. Unlike DoD, in which individual military service budgets pass through the central department, DHS components receive their appropriations directly from Congress. This lack of budgetary authority, and a general organizational structure that places decisionmaking power in the hands of components rather than a centralized headquarters, increases the complexity of the JRC's mission.

Joint Requirements Council as a New Organization

Another challenge faced by the JRC is related to the newness of the organization. The JRC is a newly formed capability at the DHS level and is to some extent still in its early implementation phase. At the same time, it is a functioning organization that carries out the activities called for by its mission, such as establishing processes and supporting the components. The entire JRC infrastructure across all of DHS is in the process of testing and refining its initial operating concepts, while also conducting analyses and identifying lessons learned that will help guide the organization's future evolution.

Scope of the Study

Given that the JRC is a relatively new organization, JRC leadership asked the Homeland Security Operational Analysis Center (HSOAC) to conduct a quick-turn review of its business processes to offer recommended actions to improve its efficacy, effectiveness, and ability to plan for the future. To accomplish these goals, this quick-turn study used a multifaceted approach to provide the JRC with the following:

- prescriptive recommendations to mitigate current and longer-term challenges to the effective and efficient execution of the JRC's roles, responsibilities, and missions
- framework and repeatable analysis approaches to continued analysis
- recommendations for subsequent deeper analysis beyond the current study.

Study Methods

This study examines JRC business processes in a multimethod approach consisting of six major steps. Table 1.1 lists and summarizes the purpose of the research steps.

Step 1: Conduct Preliminary Investigation and Review of Organizational Literature

First, we conducted a preliminary investigation and a review of organizational literature relevant to the JRC. We used the results of this review to identify broad organizational functions that correspond to the JRC's major lines of effort. Based on this preliminary investigation, we identified, assessed, and documented select JRC business processes across four primary mission areas:

- implementation and execution of the JRIMS process
- provision of requirements training to DHS component staff on the requirements process
- analysis of joint capabilities and requirements
- requirements outreach.

These mission areas are further described in Chapter Two and served as the core of the multimethod assessments described later in this section.

The preliminary exploration of the JRC led us to expect that staffing and organizational construct challenges would be the areas in greatest need of attention. Chal-

Table 1.1.
Research Steps and Purposes

Research Steps	Purpose
1. Conduct JRC preliminary investigation and review of organizational literature.	Gain contextual insights into the JRC to inform our analysis, to support the goals of identifying major functions and determining potential challenge areas.
2. Perform comparative analysis of other joint requirements councils.	Provide a summary of practices across similar joint requirements councils to identify potential lessons for the JRC. Apply lessons to the JRC context.
3. Conduct topical literature review.	Provide topical awareness on specific issues relevant to the JRC. Discuss these issues in the JRC context.
4. Hold interviews with JRC stakeholders.	Further explore and validate findings that emerged in the preceding research activities and shape prescriptive solutions.
5. Develop a JRC-specific analytic framework.	Create a systematic approach to identifying, coding, and prescribing solutions for issues facing the JRC.
6. Integrate findings to derive initial recommendations.	Provide prescriptive recommendations for current and longer-term success in JRC operations and functions.

lenges in these areas are common both in complex organizations, such as joint requirements councils, and in newly formed organizations.

Step 2: Perform Comparative Analysis of Other Joint Requirements Councils

We then reviewed literature on best practices and common pitfalls faced by other joint requirements councils. Councils examined include those serving departments of defense in the United States, Canada, the United Kingdom, Australia, and New Zealand, as well as more narrowly focused councils serving the U.S. Special Forces and Intelligence Communities. This aspect of the literature review informed our pre-interview assessments of the JRC and allowed us to capture potential lessons for the JRC. Findings from this review are presented in Chapter Three.

Step 3: Conduct Topical Literature Review

Armed with information from our preliminary investigation into the JRC and our examination of other joint council organizations, we identified focused topics for a targeted literature search. To that end, we selected literature based on problems common to complex joint council organizations:

- organizational complexity
- uncertainty
- centralized versus decentralized decisionmaking
- understaffing
- control loss.

A summary of the main literature review results is presented in Chapter Three, with further detail provided in Appendix A.

Step 4: Hold Interviews with Stakeholders

To validate our prior assessments and support recommendations tailored to the needs of the JRC, we interviewed JRC program staff about their roles and the structure of the JRC office. From these interviews, we identified challenges facing JRC staff today as well as several common concerns. The interviews and findings are discussed in Chapter Four.

Step 5: Develop a Specific Analytic Framework

We sought to develop a repeatable, systematic approach to identifying and coding issues facing the JRC. Our approach uses a Doctrine, Organization, Training, Materiel, Leadership, Personnel, Facilities Plus Regulations, Grants, and Standards (DOTMLPF+R/G/S) framework to examine JRC mission areas, identify current challenges to these efforts, and recommend potential solutions or areas in need of more-detailed future analysis.[3] The benefit of this framework is that it identifies problematic processes and also indicates methods that can improve specific management areas. While we initially considered all aspects of the framework, we found few to no analytic insights about Regulations, Grants or Standards, and therefore we omit these items from discussion. We matched challenges we encountered during our research to the actual DOTMLPF categories based on expertise in the research team in terms of both content and use of DOTMLPF as an analytic tool. Most problems fit intuitively into a category; when they did not, we used a consensus approach or sought additional counsel from experts within DHS and HSOAC to shape our selection of levers.

More detail on the definitions supporting this framework is provided in Chapter Two.

Step 6: Integrate Findings to Derive Initial Recommendations

Finally, we combined emerging insights from these methods across JRC mission areas using the DOTMLPF framework to provide near-term, functional area-based recommendations, as well as insights for future or long-term considerations.

Study Limitations

The conclusions drawn in this report should be examined with several limitations in mind. First, this report is based on a short-term study of less than three months. The quick-turn nature of the study limited the depth and breadth of the analysis. Second, many of the processes examined in this report are new and still developing as they are implemented across DHS. This report thus provides a snapshot of the JRC staff and JRIMS process at the macro level at the time of publication. Third, we did not independently verify the best practices identified among other joint councils, instead drawing on existing literature.[4] These best practices are informative for the JRC on several dimensions, but, given that DHS operates quite differently from the other organizations reviewed, caution is warranted in applying these best practices directly to the JRC. Fourth, this study does not include a full analysis of manpower and positioning requirements within the JRC. A full analysis to match staff positions descriptions to workload modeling was beyond the scope and scale of this effort. However, we do provide an assessment of staffing issues and proposed initial recommendations, based on the data available to us. Finally, this study focuses on the mission areas currently undertaken by the JRC. Should these missions change, either from an expansion of

---

[3]   See Butler et al., 2016, for an example of applying a similar version of this framework to another topic.

[4]   However, several U.S. Government Accountability Office (GAO) reports, upon which these recommendations are based, make attempts to establish best practices.

duties, from mission deprioritization, or from removal by DHS leadership, our prelimi-nary recommendations would need to be modified accordingly.[5]

Organization of This Report

The remainder of this report is organized in four chapters, with appendixes provid-ing additional detail. Chapter Two describes each of the JRC's mission areas and the framework elements that inform our analysis. Chapter Three provides a summary of literature with a focus on comparisons to other joint requirements councils and rel-evant workplace structure topics. Chapter Four discusses the results of interviews with JRC staff. Chapter Five provides a summary of emergent findings identified across other chapters. Appendix A provides additional details on relevant literature. Appendix B contains the interview protocols used for JRC staff interviews.

---

[5]   The DHS Office Inspector General is conducting an ongoing review of the JRC that may highlight additional areas of responsibility for the JRC.

CHAPTER TWO

Definitions of Mission Areas and Analytic Framework Elements

In this chapter, we describe the four JRC macro-level mission areas significant for this study. These mission areas were identified as most critical to the success of the JRC, based on a review of authoritative JRC documents, the JRC mission, and discussions with JRC subject-matter experts. The mission areas represent the tasks the JRC is mandated to perform, and are intended to capture the activities JRC staff routinely engage in as part of the DHS-wide requirements process:

- implementation and execution of the JRIMS process
- provision of training to component staff on the requirements process
- analysis of joint capabilities and requirements
- requirements outreach.

These mission areas are meant to be representative of the major lines of efforts that require JRC staff time and frame our assessments. We first define the types of activities we associate with each mission area, then we present a description of the DOTMLPF+R/G/S framework that drives our assessment.

Implementation and Execution of the JRIMS Process

The primary function of the JRC is to manage the review and validation of DHS requirements through the JRIMS process. These requirements include component specific requirements and those that are joint across components. JRIMS is still a relatively new process in DHS; as such, the impact of completing its steps is still unfolding on a case-by-case basis. JRC staff report in Acquisition Review Boards—the arenas in DHS that pass programs between Acquisition Decision Events—and note the presence or absence of validated requirements in this context. Completing the process to have validated requirements is also beginning to influence department resource allocation decisions. This process has multiple steps and involves multiple individuals across the JRC. The JRC performs the following activities for each requirements document submitted into the JRIMS process:

- **Precoordination:** The JRC front office coordinates submission of the document into the process and performs an initial review of the document for appropriateness. JRC Analysis provides an initial review to categorize the document. This can also involve precoordination with the component directly, if the component requests early feedback on a requirements document.
- **Commenting:** JRC Analysis reviews the document for alignment with criteria in the JRIMS manual and provides comments to the document sponsor.
- **Comment adjudication:** JRC Analysis works with the sponsor to adjudicate and resolve comments from across the enterprise. The JRC front office coordinates resubmission of the adjudicated document.
- **Validation recommendation:** JRC Analysis reviews the adjudicated document and provides a recommendation memo and briefing to the JRC front office.
- **Endorsement and validation:** The JRC front office engages with JRC principals (executive-level representatives from across DHS) to coordinate their endorsement of the document. The JRC director and chair validate the document. The JRC front office communicates the endorsement and validation to the sponsor and the rest of the enterprise.

To assist in managing the JRIMS process, the JRC front office also uses and oversees management of the Knowledge Management and Decision Support tool. The JRC front office also oversees any updates to the JRIMS process or manual, with input from JRC Analysis.

Requirements Training to Component Staff

JRC staff provide training on the JRIMS process to staff across DHS. Components have their own internal training as well, but the JRC is primarily responsible for providing a standardized and authoritative training on the JRIMS process. The JRC front office oversees the development and execution of all training courses offered by the JRC. Staff members from the JRC front office and JRC Analysis take turns in teaching the training courses and training sessions. The JRC is also responsible for the development and administration of a certification process for staff who receive this requirements training. We discuss the impacts of certification processes in Appendix A.

Analysis of Joint Capabilities and Requirements

The JRC oversees two efforts focusing on analysis of joint capabilities and requirements:

- The Capability Gap Assessment (CGA) assesses capability gaps from across DHS in order to create a prioritized list of unmet capabilities for the department. JRC

Analysis develops the initial list of gaps based on those identified in validated Capability Analysis Reports. JRC Analysis engages DHS-wide Portfolio Teams to assess this effort and then aggregates the assessments into a prioritized list of validated gaps. These priorities inform research and development investments, DHS strategy development, and department-wide nonmateriel changes.

- The Joint Assessment of Requirements (JAR) assesses existing programs, in both development and sustainment, in order to create an investment decision support tool. This product is one of several that inform senior leadership decisions on program funding and resourcing decisions. The precise approach to JAR is still being developed.

JRC Analysis facilitates a working group composed of stakeholders from across DHS that develops the approach and assessment criteria used by both CGA and JAR. The JAR process is currently on hold pending guidance from senior DHS leadership.

Requirements Outreach

JRC staff also engage in requirements improvement and development activities outside the JRIMS process. JRC Analysis staff offer various forms of support to components requirements staff during the development process, including informal review of documents prior to submission to JRIMS. The requirements process has historically been difficult for all types of organizations based on the level of complexity typically required. For example, the Packard Commission of 1986 found in its review of the military's acquisition process that "problems with the present defense acquisition system begin with the establishment of approved 'military requirements' for a new weapon, a step that occurs before development starts"—and/or a procurement as applicable. The Packard report also discussed the "user pull" or "technology push" drivers of requirements determination even before the requirements enter the deliberation stages for approval (Packard, 1986, p. 45). The complexity involved in the lifecycle of requirements can be increased by in the involvement of a large number of stakeholders and wide variances in the types of capabilities and items required. Like the military—which still faces challenges in processing requirements—DHS, a relatively newer organization, faces the same issues.

JRC Analysis staff also attend enterprise-wide forums related to requirements development, including Acquisition Review Teams, policy development working groups, and DHS research and development integrated product teams. JRC front office staff facilitate the JRC's external engagement by developing and maintaining the JRC website, responding to oversight bodies (e.g., GAO, DHS Office of Inspector General, congressional committees), and convening meetings of requirements stakeholders from across the department. JRC senior executives participate in many similar senior leadership forums, including Acquisition Review Boards, executive steering committees, and the chief operating officer's forum.

The work required of JRC staff in this mission area varies considerably from that in other mission areas for two reasons. First, in conducting this function, the JRC lacks the authoritative directives, policies, and processes found in other areas (e.g., the execution of JRIMS, which clearly outlines a process to be followed). Second, outreach efforts vary considerably among JRC staff as each works with different components, responds to different external requests, and participates in different committees or other meetings.

Definitions Governing DOTMLPF Frameworks

As described in Chapter One, we used a DOTMLPF framework approach to assess the four major lines of effort of the JRC. When we refer to the DOTMLPF framework throughout this report we are using the definitions described in Table 2.1. This language is based on the Defense Acquisition University's definitions and tailored to the JRC (Defense Acquisition University, 2018). We considered using an expanded frame-

Table 2.1
Adapted for the JRC Mission Areas DOTMLPF Framework Definitions

Category	Description
Doctrine	• JRC roles, responsibilities, and relationships as defined in DHS doctrine and policy, including the JRC charter, the JRIMS manual, and other relevant documents. • Other forms of authoritative documents spanning statute or law to desk guides and standing operating procedures at the local level.
Organization	• JRC organization, including the front office and analysis sections. • Organization and influence of stakeholders external to the JRC. • Organizational relationship between JRC and DHS components.
Training	• Characteristics of JRC training capabilities and execution of training events for DHS staff. • Requirements training levels among DHS component staff.
Materiel	• Effectiveness of equipment and systems in meeting JRC requirements.
Leadership	• Characteristics of JRC leadership structure in terms of roles and responsibilities of key leaders. • Leadership ability to manage, plan, and integrate JRC mission areas.
Personnel	• The availability of qualified personnel within the JRC to execute JRC functions. • Identification of personnel needs and appropriate placement of individuals with the necessary skill set.
Facilities	• The state of DHS installations, properties, and facilities and whether they effectively support JRC requirements.

SOURCE: Defense Acquisition University, 2018.

work that includes the DHS-exclusive categories of Regulations, Grants, and Standards, but found that regulations and standards have little impact on the JRC beyond what is already captured under the category of doctrine, and we found no applicable mention of grants in our assessment. Thus, we use the standard DOTMLPF categories when presenting results in this report.

In the following chapters, we combine these mission areas and framework definitions as we examine best practices among other joint council organizations, describe reviewed literature relevant to complex organizations like the JRC, and report on interviews with JRC staff members. In the final chapter, we again break out our discussion by these categories and lines of effort as we present findings and recommendations.

CHAPTER THREE

Summary of Literature Review Findings

This chapter summarizes the findings from our literature review, identifying applications and potential lessons for the JRC. In this review, we examined best practices among other joint requirements councils to serve as possible comparison points for the JRC. The review draws from previous RAND reports, the academic literature on workplace organization, and government reports on other joint councils and requirements bodies.

We further examined several workplace organization topics of concern to complex organizations like the JRC: uncertainty, decentralization of decisionmaking, understaffing, and control loss. These topics are of frequent concern to organizations with complex missions and contribute to the intricacy and complexity of the issues these types of organizations encounter.

Organizational complexity has been defined in terms of three properties: multiplicity (the number of potentially interacting organizational entities), interdependence (how connected those elements are), and diversity (degree of heterogeneity of elements) (Sargut and McGrath, 2011). The JRC fits this definition on all fronts, as it manages the requirements process for the 14 varied DHS operational and support components. Each component presents the JRC with a diverse set of missions and requirements. That said, each component is not wholly separate, as some missions have the potential for common requirements—e.g., aviation or communications equipment needs among U.S. Customs and Border Protection and the USCG—that necessitate the JRC examine requirements for interdependence across components as well.

The review has a broad scope, pulling from multiple disciplines, including economics, psychology, management, business studies, international relations, defense and security studies, and U.S. public laws and codes. A summary of the literature review findings is available in Appendix A.

Lessons from Other Joint Councils

To identify common best practices and pitfalls, we examined literature on a number of similar joint requirements councils, including:

1. the DoD Joint Requirements Oversight Council (JROC) (United States)
2. Joint Requirements Special Operations Command (United States)
3. the Independent Review Panel for Defence Acquisition (IRPDA) (Canada)
4. United Kingdom Joint Requirements Oversight Council (UK JROC)
5. Capability Acquisition and Sustainment Group (Australia)
6. Capital Equipment Acquisition (New Zealand)
7. The Joint Intelligence Community Council (JICC) (United States).

The JRC is relatively new, but other joint councils have existed for quite some time and provide examples both of best practices and potential pitfalls. General research on joint processes and organizational change also offer lessons. A recent RAND report on organizations that contest acquisition decisions found that such bodies are most effective when they are both completely independent from control of the organizations they review and integral to the acquisitions process (Cook et al., 2016). In the case of the JRC, this means that the JRC needs to be independent of DHS component control even as it is a part of DHS at large; it also must be integrated into the broader DHS acquisition processes. In a similar vein, a recent GAO report on the JRC emphasized the importance of the GAO's eight key practices for organizational transformation (GAO, 2016).[1] These practices are listed in Box 3.1.

We caution that the examples of other joint councils do not provide perfect comparisons. Most importantly, there are no perfect models: Everybody struggles to get requirements and acquisitions right (Freedberg, 2016; Locher, 2001; Macgregor, 2000;

Box 3.1: Eight Key Practices for Organizational Transformations

1. Ensure top leadership drives the transformation.
2. Establish a coherent mission and integrated strategic goals to guide the transformation.
3. Focus on a key set of principles and priorities at the outset of the transformation.
4. Set implementation goals and a timeline to build momentum and show progress from day one.
5. Dedicate an implementation team to manage the transformation process.
6. Use the performance management system to define responsibility and assure accountability for change.
7. Establish a communication strategy to create shared expectations and report related progress.
8. Involve employees to obtain their ideas and gain their ownership for the transformation (GAO, 2003, 2016).

---

[1]   The original GAO report had nine key practices, but GAO found that only eight were relevant to the JRC.

Omand, 2010; Stone, 2012; Perry, 2015; Sloan, 2013, 2014; Australian Department of Defence, 2017; Stewart and Ablong, 2013). Second, there are no joint councils quite like the JRC. Few councils are devoted solely to requirements (Cook, Nowakowski, and Unewisse, 2012), and the best example—the JROC—is orders of magnitude larger than the JRC. Still, these examples offer useful comparison points, even if not direct analogues, for the JRC.

The Joint Requirements Oversight Council

The JROC provides some lessons on how joint councils operate, in terms of both successes to emulate and problems to avoid. On the one hand, the JROC does several things right. First, its requirements process has "teeth": It is directly tied to the acquisitions and funding processes, and military sponsors have to go through the JROC (Roman and Tarr, 1998).[2] Second, it is led by someone—the vice chair of the Joint Chiefs of Staff (JCS)—who not only is high-ranking and influential but also works on behalf of a joint vision, not any individual service (Meinhart, 2010; Defense Acquisition University, 2003). Third, its constituent members are also very high ranking, ensuring that the body is accorded respect and influence (Owens, 1994). Fourth, it has large resources, in terms of both funding and manpower, along with the support of several lower bodies designed to give the JROC the expertise needed to make decisions (Owens, 1996; Lewis et al., 1998; JCS, undated). Fifth, the JROC has shrunk the size of its high-level meetings and specifically has expelled contractors from those meetings. This has allowed the JROC to discuss requirements more honestly and openly, without undue lobbying from interested contractors (Brissett, 2017).

The JROC also demonstrates several pitfalls to avoid. It has not been able to minimize acquisition costs and program overruns. GAO found that overruns have cost hundreds of billions of dollars and lasted, on average, almost two years (GAO, 2009a, 2009b). In its most recent High-Risk Report, GAO found that DoD had made progress in improving the acquisition process (GAO, 2017). The JROC must also make decisions without adequate information in the early stages of acquisition programs, a problem that challenges the acquisition process as a whole (McKernan et al., 2017).

This problem of overruns leads to and is reinforced by the second problem: The JROC has not been able to fully enforce a joint paradigm on the armed forces.[3] Many

---

[2] For the codes that govern JROC and mandate its institutional authority, see 10 U.S.C. §§ 181, 2448a, 2366a, 2366b, 2433, 2433a. For laws that govern the acquisition process, see H.R. 5013, Pub. L. 110-417, and Pub. L. 111-23. For DoD directives that govern the JROC, see DoD, 2015, and U.S. Chairman of the Joint Chiefs of Staff, undated.

[3] For one example of how a lack of jointness can lead to cost overruns, see Kavanagh et al., 2015. Kavanagh et al. perform a root cause analysis to determine the reasons behind a Nunn-McCurdy breach in the Joint Precision Approach and Landing System, finding that problems began when a civilian agency, the Army, and the Air Force abandoned the program, leaving the Navy to toil without the economy of scale that made the program fiscally viable.

researchers have stressed that the branches pay lip service to jointness before budgeting for the services' own strategic interests instead of joint priorities (Freedberg, 2016; Locher, 2001; Macgregor, 2000; Schwartz, 2010). This difficulty, even among a well-funded organization with the appropriate authorities, highlights that requirements review is a complex challenge.

The JROC has tremendous statutory power but still faces challenges. One GAO report found that the services can refuse to act in the joint interest, and combatant commanders despise a lengthy requirements process which they feel produces little added value (GAO, 2011). The JROC exercises no authority over existing programs, having little ability to impact requirements in the event new information becomes available while a program is in execution. This makes cost-saving measures extremely difficult to implement (Lewis et al., 1998). Even for joint programs, cost savings are difficult to achieve for complex programs, as adding additional stakeholders can increase the technical and programmatic challenges of program management (Drezner, Roshan, and Whitmore, 2017).

Joint Special Operations Command

The Joint Special Operations Command (JSOC) presents a possible model for the JRC, with its focus on modification to existing systems rather than new development (as is needed for many DHS components) and the speed at which it fields new capabilities.[4] That said, JSOC is extremely different from the JRC and the JROC as it receives resources differently to facilitate time-sensitive acquisition and has a high level of leadership involvement. While part of its broad purview is to set joint requirements for U.S. Special Operations Forces, its larger focus is on conducting actual combat missions as part of U.S. Special Operations Command (USSOCOM) (Priest and Arkin, 2011). In terms of acquisitions, JSOC receives most of its funding from the services, but does have its own resources under an independent appropriation, known as Major Force Program 11, that passes directly from Congress to USSOCCOM (Machina, 2014). A recent RAND report highlights the need for special forces to have a quick pathway to provide funding to meet time-sensitive missions with requirements that cannot be easily foreseen, and USSOCOM, JSOC included, possesses a speedy acquisitions process enabled by direct congressional involvement (Loredo et al., 2014; Brown, 2006).

But while JSOC demonstrates the necessity of high-level involvement to quickly cut through bureaucratic hurdles, its founding also demonstrates the limited ability of central management to impose control upon components. Congress had to pass numerous laws and give multiple clarification comments before the system was established (Paul, Porche, and Axelband, 2014). While such a system may be seen as a potential

---

[4]   A focus on modifications to existing systems should present less of a technical challenge than a purely new development program, thus reducing technical and programmatic risk. As such, these programs could be expected to be more successful than an average development program.

model for time-sensitive acquisitions (a concern of DHS components), this high-level leadership requirement places challenges on implementing this model for DHS.

The Independent Review Panel for Defence Acquisition

The IRPDA is a joint body that validates requirements in Canadian military procurement projects (Canadian Armed Forces, 2016). Like the JRC, the IRPDA is a small, relatively new body, but it differs from the JRC in two key ways. First, the IRPDA has complete independence from the bodies it reviews (IRPDA, 2016). Second, the IRPDA has direct access to expertise within the Canadian government without having to go through a central hub or product sponsors, which ensures it gets the information necessary to make validation decisions (IRPDA, 2016).

The IRPDA does face several challenges. First, Canadian acquisition efforts run into the same cost overruns and project delays that challenge U.S. efforts (Stone, 2012; Sloan, 2013). While not all overruns are the fault of the requirements process, the IRPDA was established specifically to serve as an "independent, third-party challenge function" to help control costs (Pugliese, 2015). The IRPDA has been in existence for fewer than three years, so it remains to be seen whether it will succeed in its mission. Second, while the IRPDA was created with the best of intentions, even efforts to improve requirements and reform acquisitions add another layer of bureaucracy to an already complex system (Perry, 2015). Like the first challenge, this is not a problem unique to Canada, but rather a generalized problem for requirement organizations. Third, Canadian acquisition efforts are caught between two competing priorities: buying the cheapest technology available and buying from local firms (similar to U.S. procurement restrictions based on the Federal Acquisition Regulation) (Sloan, 2014). The problem is particularly acute for Canada, given the smaller size of its defense budget and national defense industry.

UK Joint Requirements Oversight Council

The United Kingdom has recently created its own version of DoD's JROC, with the mandate to review "major project requirements at an early stage, to ensure that the performance, cost, time and risk balance is properly scrutinized and understood at the most senior levels in Defence" (UK Parliament, 2015). The UK JROC has already begun setting requirements for a new British light frigate (Allison, 2016). However, the UK JROC is too new to offer any real lessons for the JRC.[5]

---

[5]   Before establishing the UK JROC, British military requirements were handled less formally. The commander of the Joint Forces Command had been responsible for prioritizing requirements, and the Defence Audit Committee functioned—and still does—as a watchdog organization which contested acquisitions decisions (UK Ministry of Defence, 2013, 2015).

Capability, Acquisition, and Sustainment Group and Capital Equipment Acquisition

The Australian Capability, Acquisition, and Sustainment Group and New Zealand's Capital Equipment Acquisition both carry out requirements responsibilities in addition to acquisition duties more broadly (Australian Department of Defence, undated; New Zealand Defence Force, 2013). Since the two bodies are so different from the JRC in form and function, only a few lessons can be gleaned. First, jointness comes much more naturally to Australia's and New Zealand's militaries because a core requirement for both of them is interoperability with each other and with allied forces (Australian National Audit Office, 2017; New Zealand Ministry of Defence, 2016a). Second, both militaries, but New Zealand's especially, benefit from having very specific requirements spelled out from a high level (New Zealand Ministry of Defence, 2016b; New Zealand Defence Force and New Zealand Ministry of Defence, 2014; Australian Department of Defence, 2016). Of course, this is easier for a country the size of New Zealand, whose total defense budget is a fraction of the USCG's (New Zealand Defence Force and New Zealand Ministry of Defence, 2015). Given smaller budgets, each individual program can receive greater senior leader time and focus, ameliorating many of the problems faced by joint councils. Having smaller budgets also leads to a focus on more-mature systems, given a relative lack of development funds, and potentially eases the requirements process. This approach cannot be directly applied to the JRC, whose budget is significantly larger and whose senior leadership time and focus are naturally more dispersed.

The Joint Intelligence Community Council

The JICC was established in the Intelligence Reform and Terrorism Prevention Act (IRTPA) of 2004 (Pub. L. 108-458). It has numerous duties, mainly assisting the director of National Intelligence, including "advising the Director on establishing requirements, developing budgets, financial management, and monitoring and evaluating the performance of the [intelligence community]" (Office of the Director of National Intelligence, 2007).

However, the JICC provides a cautionary tale for other joint councils. It is composed entirely of high-ranking members.[6] This is normally a practice that increases the influence and effectiveness of joint councils, but the JICC's members are so high-ranking that they have little time to devote to the JICC. Indeed, the JICC meets only semiannually, giving at best a superficial glance at its long list of duties (Office of the Director of National Intelligence, 2011). Most Directors of National Intelligence (DNIs) have bypassed the JICC in favor of the Executive Committee, which is chaired by the DNI and consists of the heads of intelligence community components (Lowenthal, 2016).

---

[6]   The JICC's membership consists of the DNI, the Secretary of State, the Secretary of the Treasury, the Secretary of Defense, the Attorney General, the Secretary of Energy, the Secretary of DHS, and anybody else the President decides to mandate (50 U.S.C. § 3022).

Importantly, unlike the JICC, the Executive Committee does not have the mission of setting joint requirements (Office of the Director of National Intelligence, 2011).

In describing the difficulties of establishing a joint vision over intelligence organizations, David Omand asserts that effective change requires two preconditions:

> The first is the old adage, follow the money. Alignment of desired change and authority over the relevant budgets is essential. The second is that those who lead the process of change must have, or quickly acquire, a feel for the ethos of the organization concerned (Omand, 2010, p. 100).

For the most part, the JICC has had neither. Harknett and Stever, 2011, argue that the DNI would face challenges because IRTPA did not go far enough by making the DNI a department in and of itself, which would have given its head the requisite authority needed to centralize the intelligence community. Mike McConnell, a former DNI, wrote that the challenge of the Office of the Director of National Intelligence is "to strike the right balance between centralized direction and decentralized execution" (McConnell, 2007, p. 51). But centralized direction is meaningless without the authority to enforce it.

Summary of Joint Council Comparison

While no councils reviewed were structured exactly like the JRC, other councils did face similar sets of problems. The overwhelming lesson from other joint councils is that requirements, and acquisitions more broadly, are extremely difficult processes that no system completes perfectly. However, from the examples of these bodies, several best practices and pitfalls were identified. These best practices for joint councils revolve primarily around what can be considered organizational and leadership issues and are summarized in Table 3.1. We discuss the best practices in the JRC context specifically in the final chapter of this report, after providing additional context through our staff interviews in Chapter Four.

Best practices suggest that joint councils require authority relative to the components they review. This can be budget authority, even if it is not executed often (Harknett and Stever, 2011; Omand, 2010; Roman and Tarr, 1998), or an acknowledged ability to review existing programs (Drezner and Simpson, 2017; Lewis et al., 1998; Roman and Tarr, 1998). Budget authority need not be full control over a budget, but rather a capacity to enforce that requirements be validated before a program produces a significant number of operational units. For existing programs, this includes the ability to adapt requirements as new information becomes available during program execution. Without such authority, councils are unable to end existing programs and achieve the cost-savings goals assigned to them (Lewis et al., 1998).

Also key is the ability of joint councils to obtain information and expertise without going through the sponsor (Australian Department of Defence, 2016; New Zealand Ministry of Defence, 2016a). Collecting information in this way facilitates the

Table 3.1
Joint Requirements Council Best Practices and Pitfalls

Joint Councils Succeed When They . . .	Joint Councils Fail When They . . .
Organization	
• have budgetary authority	• lack budgetary authority
• are fully integrated into the larger acquisitions processes	• lack authority over existing programs
• have access to necessary expertise without going through sponsors	• only receive information from project sponsors
• consider jointness from the beginning of the process, not as an afterthought	• make vital decisions early in processes without adequate information
• understand the needs of components and involve them in	• do not receive buy-in from components
• limit participation in order to facilitate efficient and effective	• do not say no; requirements councils must be willing to deny validation when necessary
Leadership	
• have high-ranking leadership motivated to work on behalf of jointness when deemed appropriate	• rely upon officials who are so high-ranking that they are overwhelmed by other concerns and lack joint vision
• receive high-level attention to quicken processes and clarify specific requirements	• add layers of bureaucracy without adding value

ability of a joint council to consider jointness early in the process (Schwartz, 2010; GAO, 2012). Furthermore, joint councils need buy-in from the components they oversee and need to truly understand these components' needs. A lack of buy-in has proven harmful to many joint councils.[7] Finally, joint councils are more effective when participation is limited to the smallest number possible to facilitate efficiency and effectiveness (Brissett, 2017; Canadian Armed Forces, 2016). Joint councils, like other organizations, strike a balance between having enough participation to ensure relevant information reaches a decisionmaking body, but not having so many participants that decisionmaking is impeded. We discuss sizing issues and the balance between staffing and control loss later in this chapter.

A second key dimension visible in best practices is the role of leadership in joint council success. Leaders must be senior enough to both have a joint vision and be able to enforce it. Research has shown the JROC benefits from being led by the vice chairman of the JCS (Defense Acquisition University, 2003; Meinhart, 2010). Such high-

---

[7] See Freedberg, 2016; Harknett and Stever, 2011; Locher, 2001; Macgregor, 2000; Omand, 2010; and Schwartz, 2010, for discussion of such problems in the JICC and JROC.

level attention can lead to quicker processes and provide clarity of requirements.[8] At the same time, tapping only leaders on the most senior levels risks leaving the council spread thin as the council's business will be only one of many demands on senior leaders' time, possibly leading to backlash among senior leaders, as was seen between Combatant Commanders and the JROC (GAO, 2011; Perry, 2015). Balancing this tension is key when crafting a leadership structure of a joint council.

Summary of Workplace Structure Literature

In this section, we further examine several workplace organization topics of concern to complex organizations like the JRC: uncertainty, decentralization of decisionmaking, understaffing, and control loss. We discuss these challenges in general as they relate to complex organizations, before briefly outlining their connections to the JRC specifically.

Uncertainty

Uncertainty in the workplace can be classified into three types: job, role, and task. The latter two are most relevant to the JRC, as it undergoes role revisions and many tasks are unpredictable.

Role uncertainty "results from a lack of information and therefore missing clarity in a specific job position. This leads employees to be uncertain about their role, job objectives, and associated responsibilities" (Schmidt et al., 2014). In such an ambiguous situation, employees struggle to meet vague expectations. Role uncertainty is fundamentally subjective, so its deleterious effects are dependent on the perceptions of employee and the nature of the job. However, research has consistently shown that higher levels of role uncertainty are linked to lower performance, dissatisfaction, intentions to quit, stress, depression, and higher blood pressure (Anderson, 2006; Van Sell, Brief, and Schuler, 1981; Schuler, 1977; Rizzo, House, and Lirtzman, 1970; Tang and Chang, 2010; Ashford, Lee, and Bobko, 1989; Jackson and Schuler, 1985; Pollard, 2001; Dahl, 2011; Caplan and Jones, 1975; DiFonzo and Bordia, 1998; Schmidt et al., 2014).

Task uncertainty occurs when employees are not sure which assignments they must complete on any given day. The effects of task uncertainty are less broad-ranging than the effects of role uncertainty, but task uncertainty does lead to lower performance (Griffin, Neal, and Parker, 2007; Cooper et al., 2015). An important element of that lower performance is that task uncertainty—specifically, switching between tasks—increases the length of time required to complete tasks.

---

[8]   See Loredo et al., 2014, and Brown, 2006, for a discussion of congressional attention and the expedited acquisition process of the JSOC.

The literature identifies several actions that can be taken by managers to reduce uncertainty or ameliorate its negative effects. First, managers can reduce the frequency of organizational change (Rafferty and Griffin, 2006).[9] Importantly, it is not just the severity of change, but how often it occurs, that creates uncertainty. Indeed, in a qualitative examination of businesses, Charan and Colvin, 1999, found that effective chief executive officers (CEOs) launch relatively few major initiatives and make sure to launch new ones only when past changes have become "embedded in the company's DNA." Second, managers can carefully and openly plan for organizational change (DiFonzo and Bordia, 1998; Rafferty and Griffin, 2006). Employees who feel like there is a plan in place are less likely to panic when change does occur. Third, managers can improve communication with their employees about organizational changes and the roles of employees (Schweiger and DeNisi, 1991; DiFonzo and Bordia, 1998; Clampitt, DeKoch, and Cashman, 2000; Van Sell, Brief, and Schuler, 1981). However, one scholar argues that one-way communication, though vital, is not enough, and instead contends that employees must also be allowed to communicate their thoughts and concerns to management (Bordia et al., 2004).

Fourth, managers can work to create a culture of trust among staff and between staff and management (DiFonzo and Bordia, 1998). Fifth, management can provide expert advisers to employees (Keith, Demirkan, and Goul, 2017). Keith, Demirkan, and Goul found that a positive effect of uncertainty is that it increases the willingness of employees to seek advice, which is associated with higher productivity.

Sixth, managers can involve employees in decisionmaking, which serves to empower them (Wall, Cordery, and Clegg, 2002; Prendergast, 2002; Cordery et al., 2010; Leifer and Mills, 1996). Indeed, empowering staff was a key recommendation in a recent RAND study on agile acquisition (Drezner and Simpson, 2017). In the literature on business science and management, decentralization, delegation, and empowerment have long been buzz words. However, these practices do not work for all business environments; they only improve employee productivity in uncertain workplaces in which close managerial supervision makes less sense.

Centralized Versus Decentralized Decisionmaking

As highlighted above, employee involvement in (decentralized) decisionmaking offers one way to reduce uncertainty. Much of the academic literature on organizational decisionmaking focuses on private companies deciding between implementing centralized or decentralized procedures. Acemoglu et al., 2007, find that decentralization is preferable when there is an information imbalance, that is, when constituent parts have better information than central management. Similarly, Graham, Harvey, and

---

[9] For the JRC in particular, reducing organizational change should be beneficial because frequent change has hampered the ability of contractors to work with the government (U.S. House Committee on Armed Services, 2012).

Puri, 2015, find that CEOs specifically are more likely to delegate when they have less personal knowledge and greater need for information. Both findings support the literature's recommendation that uncertainty be mitigated by delegation of some decision-making and authority to those who have the best information access.

Understaffing

The literature describes staffing on a continuum ranging from *understaffed* to *overstaffed*. Originally, much of the research on understaffing focused on the short-term, positive effects: Understaffing can boost motivation and creativity in teams, increase willingness to listen to diverse viewpoints, make members feel more involved, increase team effectiveness, and lower costs, through both lower payroll and lower costs of coordination in smaller teams (Weiss and Hoegl, 2016; Arnold and Greenberg, 1980; Wicker et al., 1976; Campion, Papper, and Medsker, 1996; Kessler, 2000). In teams that are understaffed, team members feel the need to band together and work harder to make up for their smaller numbers.

However, some studies have disputed these positive findings (Ganster and Dwyer, 1995; Mani, Kesavan, and Swaminathan, 2015). More importantly, there is broad agreement in the literature that chronic understaffing has intense harmful effects on employees, including stress, burnout, depression, reduced motivation, and lower performance (Hudson and Shen, 2015; Ganster and Rosen, 2013). Understaffing also reduces conformance quality, which is how well employees carry out central management directives and standard operating procedures (Ton, 2008). When workplaces face a labor shortage, employees cut corners to compensate for being understaffed, which dramatically reduces product quality (Oliva and Sternman, 2001).

Control Loss and Optimal Organization Size

Related to understaffing is control loss, which refers to the dilution of control that central management has over the components of an organization. The primary finding from the literature on control loss is that, when organizations grow, there is a trade-off between increasing the number of employees and decreasing management's control over them (Williamson, 1967). In effect, organizations are like a game of "telephone," with each additional layer of hierarchy increasing the chance that central management's message will be unclear. While efforts to apply control loss to specify the precise optimal size of an organization have run into difficulties (see Evans, 1975, for an example of how modeling assumption can dramatically alter the predicted optimal number of employees), the literature on control loss does offer several useful conclusions. In general, organizations that have less time to make decisions and that employ higher-quality individuals as decisionmakers tend to have smaller optimal sizes (Gradstein, Nitzan, and Paroush, 1990). Regardless of the number of levels of hierarchy, control loss, much like uncertainty, can be reduced through effective communication and trust (Narayanaswamy, Grover, and Henry, 2013).

Conclusions from the Literature

The literature offers several relevant conclusions for the JRC. First, other joint councils offer examples of best practices to emulate and potential pitfalls to avoid. These best practices are largely organizational, suggesting that joint councils operating in an organizational structure that grants them authority over the components they review are more successful than those in other organizational structures. Given that the JRC lacks such authority, negative outcomes common to complex organizations could result. Two key sources of concerns are uncertainty and understaffing.

Workplace environments characterized by uncertainty to the degree that role conflict occurs (see Rizzo, House, and Lirtzman, 1970; Schmidt et al., 2014) are harmful to employee well-being and productivity. Such uncertainty could develop in the JRC given the decentralized nature of decisionmaking within the DHS requirements process, and within DHS as a whole. With the component-driven nature of DHS, staff at central organizations like the JRC may experience significant task uncertainty. Prolonged understaffing, a possible issue in many complex organizations, also reduces employee productivity and hurts employee morale. As the JRC matures and the demands placed on it change, staffing levels must be watched and periodically analyzed to avoid these negative impacts. We examine these factors in more detail in Chapter Four, through interviews with JRC staff.

Joint Requirements Council Staffing Interviews

To better understand current JRC processes and their impacts on staff, we conducted interviews with 12 JRC staff members.[1] These interviews primarily examined four topics:

- the details of staff positions
- the processes staff contribute to
- the people with whom the staff coordinate to accomplish their tasks
- any challenges that might arise during staff duties.

These topics were selected based on our review of authoritative documents, the business processes documented in Chapter Two, and conversations with JRC subject-matter experts. The purpose of these topics was to provide greater insight into the details of individual staff positions and to facilitate our understanding of connections and challenges across positions and processes.

We examined each interview for common themes and challenges, and discuss in depth four themes that were mentioned by the majority of staff:

- changes in staff structure over time
- the efforts that JRC staff focus on
- the influence of components in the requirements process
- uncertainty among JRC staff (which corroborated the need for this discussion in the related literature discussion in Chapter Three).

More detail on the interview methodology is available in Appendix B.

---

[1] These 12 staff members represent the entire JRC staff available for interviews at the time of this study. We interviewed four JRC personnel in leadership positions, four JRC analysts, and four JRC front office personnel. Interviews took place in November 2017, and were primarily conducted in person at the JRC office (except as required by staff schedules). Given the small size of the staff, we do not provide numeric estimates for each statement or specific quotations to avoid identifying interview subjects. Nevertheless, we are confident in these general trends, as no item reported in this chapter was mentioned by fewer than three-quarters of applicable staff.

Interview Findings

The current staffing level and structure of the JRC, combined with the component-dependent nature of JRC work, leaves staff reacting to external events and with less time for executing longer-term, enterprise-wide objectives. To the extent that the JRC is intended to be forward looking and focus on requirements with an enterprise-wide view, as opposed to a component-centric view, staffing changes may be warranted.

It should be noted that these conclusions are drawn from subjective interviews with JRC staff and an understanding of the organization's changing workload and structure over the past year, not formal analyses of time usage. JRC staffing needs to be examined with more rigor, via a formal micro-level workforce analysis to align work flow, organization, business processes, metrics of success, and required staffing capabilities. Based on currently available data, we are unable to offer a recommendation as to the type of staff (analyst or front office) that should be increased or how responsibilities for enterprise-wide requirements activities should be distributed between staff to maximize organizational effectiveness. The discussion that follows should be understood in this context. That being said, we do offer preliminary macro-level recommendations on how staffing increases could be distributed, based on our assessments in Chapter Five.

We categorized our interview findings into the four themes shown above and discuss each individually below.

Staff Structure Has Changed Substantially Over the Past Year

Based on our interviews, including with staff who have been with the JRC from its beginnings, the JRC is currently staffed primarily by government employees—a significant change from the summer and fall of fiscal year (FY) 2016. Before this, the JRC front office was primarily staffed by personnel detailed from DHS components, with other staff functions executed by contractor support staff, including FFRDC analysis of early documents. Starting roughly in November 2016, the JRC shifted to a staff of predominantly government employee analysts as the JRC Analysis section was staffed up.

JRC's focus also has shifted to analysis of current requirements documents, rather than analysis of longer-term planning functions traditionally associated with a PMO. Some of this change occurred as the JRC matured and moved from planning to executing its activities, but several interview subjects noted potential weaknesses as well. Multiple interview subjects, including long-time JRC staff, noted that they found the organization to be "reactive" due to limited staff time. Although the JRC can meet its demands with its current level of staffing, doing so leaves little slack in the system and results in an organization that tends to be focused on the day's tasks and emergent issues. As such, future planning and strategic activities, once the focus of the organization, have been deprioritized in favor of responding to the issues of the moment.

While current staffing appears sufficient to meet existing demands, this is likely to change as more and more requirements need to be reviewed by JRC staff. Using the data available to us, we found that the number of documents submitted through the JRIMS process has increased—with roughly four documents per month submitted in FY 2016, compared to eight documents per month in FY 2017.[2] Figure 4.1 presents a graphical representation of the documents received per month (dashed lines) compared to the relative number of analysts and front office or PMO staff per document (solid green and red lines). These lines divided the number of program staff in each section by the total number of JRIMS documents received that month. This is an approximate measure of JRIMS related workload, and indicates that JRC staffing levels have increased in the past year at a rate consistent with document throughput from components.

In general, JRC staffing has been sufficient to maintain the relative ratio of staff per document received, but this assessment is limited by two factors. First, this analysis did not consider documents by type or complexity. However, although this study did not include an analysis of projected JRIMS workflow, multiple interview subjects noted the increasing complexity of documents being submitted, as components become more familiar with the JRIMS process and develop their own requirements

Figure 4.1
JRIMS Documents and JRC Staffing Changes Over Time

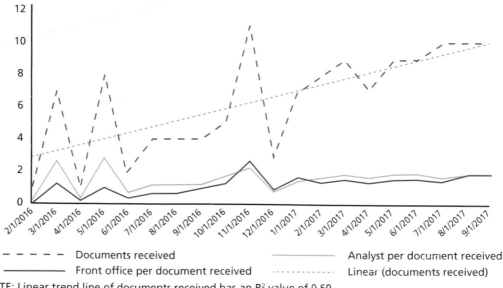

NOTE: Linear trend line of documents received has an R^2 value of 0.50.
RAND RR2473-4.1

---

[2]   Based on HSOAC analysis of JRC performance data. FY 2016 data begin in February of that year. JRC performance data are maintained by HSOAC and track each document received by the JRC, including its type, component of origin, and time spent in each stage of the JRIMS process.

workforce. Should this trend continue, it is likely these documents will require additional staff time, further limiting the JRC's ability to be forward-looking or focus on enterprise-wide functions. Second, this assessment of staffing per document does not account for work beyond the JRIMS process that JRC staff engage in; we discuss this point further below.

Staff Are Simultaneously Focused on Multiple Related But Separate Efforts

Interviews with the JRC staff revealed that the JRC is conducting several efforts simultaneously, including processing JRIMS requirements documents and working to establish a requirements community within DHS components. While the bulk of staff time is devoted to the mission area related to JRIMS, many JRC staff are also drawn into the other mission areas as defined in Chapter Two. The JRIMS manual (DHS, 2016) establishes strict timelines for document staffing, so reviewing and managing these documents can take up much of an analyst's time. Time spent on JRIMS tasks varies by position and individual and can vary from week to week as the flow of documents changes. JRIMS is not the only task JRC staff focus on, as all JRC staff also report undertaking some activities to support the establishment of a requirements community within DHS.

Establishing a requirements community within DHS involves both training and a change in mindset, and the JRC works to facilitate both for DHS. JRC staff dedicate time to training personnel from DHS components through established training courses and component-level interactions. These courses are created by the JRC, managed by JRC staff, and have JRC staff dedicating considerable time as instructors. The JRC also has a training officer, who coordinates with staff from both the analysis team and the PMO team. At least one staff member from each team is present at each training.

Beyond formal training, JRC analysts report individual meetings with the components for which they are responsible for discussing analyses that need to be performed or other steps that need to be undertaken before a document can be submitted through JRIMS. These more-informal interactions also help educate component staff on the realities and necessity of the requirements process.

JRC staff also report attending numerous working groups, councils, and other decision forums to provide a JRC presence. We refer to these activities more generally as "requirements outreach." JRC staff attend these events to influence broader DHS decisionmaking toward a "requirements-focused mindset," which refers to analysis and thinking that prioritizes meeting capability needs rather than starting with an acquisition-based solution already determined. Because significant focus on requirements is new to DHS, this process is unfolding slowly, but increasing over time. Components vary considerably in their level of requirements maturation, with some well-established in their requirements thinking and others still adopting the concept as the JRC was stood up. The development of this mindset across DHS is a primary element of the JRC mission and receives considerable staff time and resources as a result.

Given its current mission and responsibilities, both projects are necessary for the JRC to be successful in the long run, but currently provide limitations for the office overall and individual staff. JRC staff involved with JRIMS must constantly balance their limited time between reviews of documents and attending other meetings. This demand will only increase as the JRIMS process matures and documents become more complex.

Processes Are Dominated by Component, Not Joint, Requirements

The JRC primarily processes individual component requirements, with few that could be considered "joint" requirements. This is largely due to the JRIMS process being "component-led and component-driven." This is not a unique characteristic of JRIMS, but rather one part of the larger decentralized nature of DHS, which vests considerable authority and budgetary decisions in the hands of its components creating a decentralized organizational culture in which decisionmaking power rests with operational components, not a central headquarters.

This structure gives components the responsibility for submitting requirements and conducting analysis of their own requirements, as well as control over the content and timing of their submissions. This includes components not being bound by response deadlines laid out in the JRIMS manual for their steps of the JRIMS process. While the JRC is bound to react to documents in the process on a set schedule, components are afforded complete flexibility to work the schedule as they chose. JRC analysts are assigned to specific components to gain required subject-matter expertise on the unique aspects of different DHS components. This assignment helps analysts develop a deeper understanding of component-specific requirements and needs, but does little to aid efforts to view requirements jointly since no one JRC analyst has a view over all functionally equivalent requirements. At least some analyst time is currently dedicated to functional,[3] rather than component-based, requirements review, but this is the exception rather than the rule. Other efforts to view requirements with an enterprise-wide view, notably the JAR, have been conducted by JRC staff but are currently on hold pending direction from senior DHS leadership.

Staff Report Substantial Uncertainty in Their Work

JRC staff report having little certainty regarding their work and limited control over their own schedules. Interview subjects frequently stated that the only thing they were certain of is that they would soon be responding to some currently unknown demand on their time, but they had little to no ability to predict what this demand would be,

---

[3] By *functional*, we mean the practice of assigning analysis for all requirements executing a similar function— e.g., all aviation—rather than assigning analysis based on component of origin.

even a few days in advance. This uncertainty is driven by the factors discussed above—a largely reactive-focused organization managing a component-led and component-driven process. This component focus, combined with a need to represent the JRC broadly beyond the JRIMS process, leaves JRC staff little ability to predict when documents will come in, or what meetings will be added to their schedule. Interview subjects noted that some components precoordinated the submission of documents, allowing them more certainty in upcoming workload, but this was regarded as the exception rather than the rule. Furthermore, while precoordination makes JRIMS work more predictable, it adds an additional review step, which increases workload and also has uncertain timing and expectations. While this uncertainty is not unexpected given the decentralized nature of DHS, should it persist in the long run it could have several negative consequences for the JRC, as discussed earlier in Chapter Three.

Summary of Interviews

The primary challenge facing JRC today involves personnel: Specifically, our interviews indicate that the JRC is an understaffed organization, given the complexity and diversity of its current functions and the DHS-wide effort to view requirements through a joint process. It may be possible for DHS leadership to address these issues without adding additional staff to the JRC by reducing JRC workload. This could be done by limiting the number of documents that pass through the JRIMS or ending JRC outreach efforts. As these examples appear to be against the grain of current DHS efforts to move toward more joint requirements we focus our discussion on staffing levels.

The JRC is attempting to simultaneously complete multiple related, but distinct, missions. According to those we interviewed, the two taking up the most staff time are processing current component-level requirements, and guiding requirements analysis and generation across the broader DHS enterprise. Interviews with JRC staff suggest that the organization is staffed to a level and structure that allow it to meet the needs of current component requirements, but not fully work toward an enterprise-wide view. JRC staff can meet the needs of the JRIMS process and react to other demands placed on them, but have few additional resources to plan for or undertake longer-term strategic or enterprise-wide efforts. As the demands of document reviews appear poised to continue to increase over time, having on average per month doubled in FY 2017 compared with those in the first year of JRIMS implementation—and, given the importance of broader enterprise-wide efforts to the JRC mission, additional staff resources are required for the JRC to successfully execute both efforts. Additionally, two front-office personnel have recently left the office and have not yet been replaced. Other JRC staff are currently back filling these positions, further stretching already limited staff time.

The JRC also faces two other issues related to staffing, but largely stemming from an organizational source. These challenges are driven by the relationship between DHS components and the JRC. The first is the high degree of uncertainty staff face in conducting their work. This uncertainty is largely driven by the component-dominated nature of the JRIMS process and DHS more broadly, and thus beyond the ability of the JRC to fully change. One change that would increase JRC authority and help with staff uncertainty is to give the JRC additional authority over the timing and responsiveness of components during the JRIMS process. Any efforts the JRC could make to give more stability to staff schedules would be beneficial in the long run. As shown in Chapter Three, there are several steps recommended by the literature to reduce the negative impacts of uncertainty. Such steps include communicating with and listening to JRC staff concerns over uncertainty and involving employees in decisionmaking through delegation, actions that could benefit the JRC even if other steps would prove more difficult in the government context.

The second issue involves a tension in how the program should be structured. As currently organized, the program allows analysts to develop expertise and relationships with components by assigning them to all requirements for a given component. This arrangement serves the component-driven nature of requirements well, but does little to foster jointness in requirements analysis. Alternative organizations, perhaps with some analysts assigned functionally and other staff serving as liaisons to components, might lead to an increased ability to consider joint requirements across the enterprise, but may also require considerably more staff resources than exist in the program today.

CHAPTER FIVE

Summary of Emergent Findings

In this study, we conducted a multimethod assessment of JRC mission areas. To perform this assessment, we examined literature on best practices among other joint councils, reviewed academic literature on key struggles facing complex organizations like the JRC, and interviewed JRC staff to better understand the challenges they face. This chapter combines the insights gained from these efforts, using a JRC-specific DOTMLPF framework to present emergent findings and indicate areas requiring additional attention as the JRC continues to mature. Overall, we conclude that challenges to the JRC's efforts—across multiple mission areas—arise from the organizational relationship between the JRC and DHS components and from the staffing levels required to execute tasks across all mission areas.

We present our summary assessment of JRC DOTMLPF categories by mission area in Table 5.1. We assessed each DOTMLPF and mission area combination, based on the challenges identified in previous chapters. We matched challenges we encountered during our research to DOTMLPF categories based on our team's expertise with

Table 5.1
Summary of JRC DOTMLPF Categories by Mission Area

Category	JRIMS	Requirements Training	Joint Analysis	Outreach
Doctrine				
Organization				
Training				
Materiel				
Leadership				
Personnel				
Facilities				

NOTE: Green = no challenge noted during assessment; amber = minor issue: addressing would produce positive benefits for JRC staff; red = major issue: should be addressed immediately to ameliorate negative impacts on JRC efficiency and/or effectiveness.

both the content and the use of the DOTMLPF as an analytic tool. Most problems fit intuitively into a category; when they did not, the research team used a consensus approach or sought additional counsel from experts within DHS and RAND.

We considered best practices and problems found in other joint council organizations, a review of organizational literature, and interviews with JRC staff. Given the differences between the JRC and other organizations, we gave additional weight to JRC staff interviews. We ranked a combination "green" if we noted no challenge in our assessments. We coded a combination "amber" if we noted only a minor challenge. (Minor challenges are those that do not stop or significantly impede staff from conducting their work; JRC and DHS leadership should be aware of these challenges and address them as time and resources allow.)

We coded a combination "red" if it presented a major challenge to the JRC. Major challenges are defined as those that either stop JRC staff from working on a function or present a significant impediment to their work. Unlike minor challenges, these challenges currently have a negative impact on JRC efficiency and effectiveness, according to staff interviews, and should be addressed as soon as possible.

Based on our analysis, the categories of Materiel and Facilities did not present challenges to the JRC at this time and are not discussed. We discuss the other categories in more detail below.

Doctrine

The JRC faces few challenges with doctrine, as JRC doctrine appears to be properly reflected in key documents, such as the JRIMS manual. Multiple interview subjects noted that the JRIMS manual clearly indicates how their work is to be conducted and can be used to answer questions that arise in the course of their tasks. The one challenge we note in this area is that formal doctrine says little to nothing in the area of requirements outreach. This omission poses a challenge, as this mission area was described as key by multiple senior members of the JRC—who emphasized their work to establish a "requirements culture" within DHS as a whole as vital to the organization. Also, many staff members reported spending a plurality, if not an outright majority, of their time on tasks in this mission area. Given its centrality to the organization as a whole, a lack of authoritative documentation on what exactly the JRC is trying to establish, and how staff should go about doing so, poses a challenge. More-detailed expectations in this area from DHS leadership could better convey to DHS components what is required of them and help JRC staff prioritize their day-to-day activities across mission areas. The establishment of high-level goals and priorities for the organization in this area would provide clearer guidelines to JRC staff as they balance the demands of the various functions the JRC performs.

Organization

The JRC faces significant challenges based on the nature of its relationship to DHS components. JRC mission areas are based on a "component-led and component-driven" requirements process. As a result of the decentralized nature of requirements decision-making within DHS, JRC staff face considerable uncertainty in their work. Because components drive the requirements process, they impose demands on JRC staff that those within the program have a limited ability to control. Many interview subjects expressed the sentiment that the only certain aspect of their work was uncertainty. Literature links such significant uncertainty to such processes as understaffing, which can lead to lower employee well-being and satisfaction and decreased job performance. Furthermore, vesting increased authority in the JRC over the requirements process would fall in line with best practices identified among other joint requirements councils and could improve JRC effectiveness and efficiency in addition to any benefits provided to staff. Specifically, the JRC currently lacks any budget authority or authority over existing programs, and receives most of its information from the component sponsor of a requirement. For example, the authority to review existing programs is associated with an increased ability to achieve cost-savings goals (Lewis et al., 1998) while access to information independent of a sponsor is key to facilitating jointness in requirements (Schwartz, 2010; GAO, 2012). This is not to say that the JRC should control the budgetary or acquisition processes, but rather that requirements play a role in those efforts as well. For budgets, this could include requiring a validated requirement as a prerequisite for the program to deliver major quantities to the field. For access to existing programs, this would include an ability to review program requirements as a program evolves over its lifecycle or as new information becomes available.[1] A JRC with more-robust authority over joint requirements, including over component actions, would improve JRC effectiveness, increase the JRC's ability to view requirements with an enterprise-wide perspective, and reduce the task uncertainty imposed on JRC staff. Because joint requirements are central to the JRC's mission, this challenge should be addressed as soon as possible.

Training

The level of requirements training among DHS component staff poses a challenge for JRC staff in the mission areas addressing JRIMS and requirements outreach. In both areas, staff noted significant disparities by DHS component or headquarters elements in the level of requirements training staff had received. This lack of staff training on the

---

[1]   An ability to review requirements on existing programs, especially those that predate the JRC's stand up, would also facilitate existing efforts to establish joint requirements across DHS components, as the JRC would not be limited to requirements requiring new validations when examining possibilities for jointness across DHS.

DHS component end requires JRC staff to spend significant amounts of time helping them craft requirements documents. This situation was noted to be improving with the continued use of the JRIMS process, but several components still have a limited number of personnel trained to address requirements, and the lack of training among some DHS component staff continues to impose challenges on the JRC.

Leadership

Leadership presents few challenges to the JRC staff. The one exception of note is in the mission area of joint requirements analysis. This dimension was noted as a potential challenge. All staff who discussed this mission area indicated that the JRC could conduct joint analysis, but noted that the cross-component nature of this work would require support from senior leadership within the department to be executed. Given recent leadership changes in the department at the time of this report, this effort was noted as "on hold" until further leadership guidance could be obtained. Obtaining such guidance as quickly as possible will determine whether this mission area will be prioritized.

Personnel

According to interviews with staff, the JRC faces significant staffing challenges across all mission areas. We conclude that the JRC is understaffed, given the breadth of its responsibilities. Staffing has increased as the JRIMS process demands have increased, but not at a pace required to fully meet all demands placed on the JRC staff. JRC staffing increases, primarily in the analysis section, have been sufficient to keep pace with the increased volume of JRIMS documents submitted, but interview subjects indicated this has done little to help them address demands placed on their time in other mission areas. This tension is felt across mission areas: The JRC currently lacks even a single full-time staff member dedicated to training, has limited analyst time for joint requirements analysis, and requires the majority of its staff to balance the needs of keeping to the deadlines established in the JRIMS manual with their outreach responsibilities. As discussed in Chapter Three, literature suggests that understaffing can lead to a "pulling together effect;" team members work harder to make up for their small numbers in the short run, but, in the long run, employee well-being, satisfaction, and ability to sustain high work quality are negatively affected. To avoid these negative effects and ensure that effective review of requirements and outreach to the broader DHS community continues, this challenge should be addressed as soon as possible.

Preliminary Recommendations

While we have described several challenges to the JRC overall, we find that the JRC faces two major challenges today that we recommend be addressed in the near term. The JRC's current organizational and personnel systems lack the staff needed to accomplish all tasks across its mission areas, and the JRC's staff faces a high degree of uncertainty in their work, given the decentralized nature of decisionmaking in the DHS requirements process. According to staff interviews, these challenges are negatively affecting the efficacy and effectiveness of the JRC and should be addressed as soon as possible.

Further analysis beyond the scope of this project would be required to determine exact staffing levels and the types of staff (e.g., analysis, PMO) that would be most effective. This analysis of micro-level staffing concerns would need to link job duties, organizational workload, metrics of success, and the larger mission of the JRC to determine the most effective staffing levels and mix.[2] As a preliminary step to aid this effort, we offer recommendations for approximate staffing increases by mission area, based on our macro-level assessments to address major gaps in the implementation journey to date.

We make two primary recommendations to address these major challenges based on insights gained from this preliminary study.

First, **we recommend DHS further consider and analyze an increase in JRC staffing above current staff and contractor support levels to better cover all JRC mission areas.** Additional staff are necessary to avoid the negative impacts of understaffing and to ensure that the JRC is able to continue its efforts to build a requirements community within DHS more broadly. Without such a community, an enterprise-wide requirements process is unlikely to gain the component buy-in that is required to make such organizations successful. Staffing increases are best accomplished as a result of manpower analysis or another scientifically rigorous means of determining needs. With the JRC still evolving as a newly formed organization, it is also important to note that workload demands will continue to emerge and/or transform and JRC stakeholders should be prepared to assess and act to meet those demands.

As an interim solution to use before a detailed manpower analysis can be performed, we offer a preliminary yet systematic approach that estimates each major challenge (red coding in Table 5.1) as requiring 0.75 FTE to address, with each minor challenge (amber coding in Table 5.1) requiring 0.25 FTE to address. Doing so suggests

---

[2] No assessment is offered here on the types of staff (e.g., contractors versus government employees) that could be hired to address these needs. Such distinctions would be part of a formal manpower analysis linking organizational mission, tasks, position descriptions, and projected workload.

an increase of JRC staff by seven FTE.[3] We recommend the following increases of staff time by mission areas.[4]

1. **Implementation and execution of the JRIMS process:** To keep the documents-to-analyst ratio consistent with prior levels (see Figure 4.1), **the JRC will require an additional two analysts** to keep pace with anticipated increases in document review demands. This assumes that documents submissions from components continue at a similar rate (which we have no reason to doubt), but does not address the increasing complexity of document submission noted by multiple interview subjects.

2. **Provision of requirements training to component staff on the requirements process:** Training component staff in requirement analysis is vital to the establishment of a requirements community within DHS and should continue to be supported with staff time to the extent possible. Currently this function is coordinated by one staff member whose time is split between other front office duties as a result of two recent staff departures. **We recommend the addition of two front office staff members to replace those exits** and allow for a full-time staffer dedicated to training coordination and development of a certification for requirements training.

3. **Analysis of joint capabilities and requirements:** If analysis with an expressly department-wide, rather than component-centric, view is to be a JRC focus, this mission area requires at least two analysts (one for the capability gap analysis and one for the joint requirements plus front office support) worth of staff time as it involves a considerable level of effort in both analysis and outreach. Currently this effort does not receive one full FTE of analyst time. As such if DHS leadership wishes to make this aspect of the JRC mission a priority, **one additional analyst billet** is warranted.

4. **Requirements outreach:** This mission area faces the most challenges noted in our assessment, and as such requires additional staff to address them. How these staff could best be assigned would need to be determined by future analysis, but two possible examples present themselves. First, the JRC could continue with a

---

[3]   We considered other notional numeric assignments but settled on these, given their rough approximation to other observed staffing factors emergent from our data. For example, two recent front office departures' impact on training and the JRIMS documents-to-analyst levels. As such, we consider this a useful macro-level estimate and starting point, but admit that an ideal number of staff could be lower or higher than this estimate.

[4]   One possible method to meet this staffing increase if additional billets cannot be assigned directly to the JRC is through the use of liaison personnel assigned to JRC from the components. These component personnel, assigned to the JRC for a period of two to three years, could bring component specific expertise to the JRC and when they return back to the component provide additional requirements analysis experience gained during their time at the JRC. These liaisons have the potential to increase cohesion between JRC and component efforts in the long term. This possibility faces challenges, as already noted many components have relatively few requirements staff already, further stretching their own operations if they remove them to support the JRC.

larger version of its existing division of labor and add these staff to the analysis or front-office staff based on the type of outreach deemed most critical (component or otherwise, respectively). As another alternative, the JRC could reorganize its outreach in a matrix-based approach (see Kerzner, 2003, for a description of matrix versus functionally based organizations). This organization would have one set of staff dedicated to component outreach, and a separate staff who conduct analysis by function or JRIMS portfolio team rather than by component as is done today. Assessing costs, benefits, and risks between these two alternatives would require additional detailed manpower analysis. Regardless of the organizational approach, requirements outreach is a key effort of the JRC and should be supported with additional staff time. **This preliminary analysis indicates the need for approximately two additional FTEs.**

Summing the personnel recommendations listed above, we suggest that a total of seven additional FTE of staff for the JRC be considered to address the challenges described above. Additional analysis staff would allow the JRC to more fully engage with complex documents and develop expertise with a component's requirements, while additional front office staff would support other JRC efforts that enhance the effort to establish a broader requirement community within DHS.[5]

Second, **we recommend that the department further examine possible changes to the organizational relationship between the JRC and the DHS components.** The current arrangement, with little JRC authority over components, presents several challenges, as we have discussed in our assessment. The lack of any authority to link validated requirements to budgets, insight into existing programs, or ability to obtain outside information runs counter to several of the best practices established by other joint requirement council organizations and hinders the ability of JRC to effect cost savings or more fully consider joint requirements. More concretely, our interviews indicate that components impose significant uncertainty on JRC staff members as the driving force of the JRIMS process. Any efforts the JRC can take to plan for this uncertainty or otherwise provide stability to employees' schedules would be beneficial. Initial steps supported by our assessment that could be undertaken in this area include more systematically linking the validation of requirements to the production of significant numbers of operational units, and allowing the JRC to review existing programs as circumstances change. Reviews of best practices among joint council organizations suggest that these steps, along with the high-level leadership present at the JRC, will improve the organizational effectiveness and efficiency.

The exact details of a new organizational arrangement would require further analysis of each component's requirements processes. Such analysis was beyond the scope

---

[5] Note that current assessments assume similar levels of HSOAC contactor support to analysis efforts as was present in FY 2017. Should this change, the required staff to support JRC analysis efforts would also change.

of this effort but could be conducted using the framework described in this report to facilitate comparisons to JRC processes. While the underlying relationship between components and the JRC is unlikely to change in the short term, ultimately moving to a system with greater central authority over requirements decisionmaking will facilitate the success of a JRC-led enterprise-wide requirements process. Barring this, efforts to formalize the partnership between the JRC and DHS components in authoritative documents would offer some benefit to DHS.

Literature Review

This appendix summarizes the findings from literature relevant to the JRC staff. It draws from previous RAND reports, the academic literature on workplace organization, and government reports on other joint councils and requirements bodies. The review has a broad scope, pulling from multiple disciplines, including economics, psychology, sociology, management, business studies, international relations, defense and security studies, and U.S. public laws and codes.

Workplace Structure Literature

The study of what makes workplaces function best and what factors affect employees' ability to do work is large and ongoing. Various concepts have been analyzed for how they affect employees, from uncertainty to decisionmaking structures to understaffing.

Uncertainty

Uncertainty for employees is classified into three types: job uncertainty, role uncertainty, and task uncertainty (the latter two are generally called role ambiguity and task ambiguity). Job uncertainty refers to an employee feeling a lack of security in his or her future employment status.

Large-scale organizational change often leads to job uncertainty, even if no direct changes to an employee's role are made (Dahl, 2011; Schweiger and DeNisi, 1991; Rafferty and Griffin, 2006; DiFonzo and Bordia, 1998). Intuitively, this makes sense as mergers, acquisitions, and the like often lead to layoffs (Siegel and Simons, 2010). Job uncertainty is also caused by job relocation (Moyle and Parks, 1999).

Job uncertainty leads to job dissatisfaction and intentions to leave (Rafferty and Griffin, 2006; Nelson, Cooper, and Jackson, 1995). Intentions to leave are especially troubling as employee turnover drastically reduces productivity (Gans, Koole, and Mandelbaum, 2003). Employees who are constantly wondering whether they will be given a pink slip naturally start to look elsewhere for employment and consequently have less time to devote to their current positions. Job uncertainty is linked with higher blood pressure and stress (Pollard, 2001).

Role uncertainty occurs when an employee is not certain what exactly his or her job entails or what performance is expected by his or her boss. Role uncertainty is caused by bad management practices, particularly by poor guidance given from managers (Van Sell, Brief, and Schuler, 1981; Rizzo, House, and Lirtzman, 1970). One scholar also argues that a poor fit between the complexity of tasks, technology, and structure—that is, having a simple hierarchical management structure governing a role with complex tasks and technology—also leads to role uncertainty (Schuler, 1977).

Literature suggests that role uncertainty is even more damaging than job uncertainty. It is linked to lower performance (Anderson, 2006; Van Sell, Brief, and Schuler, 1981; Schuler, 1977; Rizzo, House, and Lirtzman, 1970; Tang and Chang, 2010), dissatisfaction and intentions to quit (Ashford, Lee, and Bobko, 1989; Jackson and Schuler, 1985; Van Sell, Brief, and Schuler, 1981; Schuler, 1977; Rizzo, House, and Lirtzman, 1970; Tang and Chang, 2010), stress and depression (Dahl, 2011; Caplan and Jones, 1975; Jackson and Schuler, 1985; Van Sell, Brief, and Schuler, 1981; Schuler, 1977; Rizzo, House, and Lirtzman, 1970; DiFonzo and Bordia, 1998; Schmidt et al., 2014), and higher blood pressure (Pollard, 2001). If employees are not certain what is expected of them, they naturally struggle to meet those vague expectations.

Task uncertainty occurs when employees are not certain of the various assignments they must complete on any given day. Importantly, this is separate from (although related to) role uncertainty; it is possible for an employee to be certain of his or her role but not of the individual tasks he or she must accomplish ahead of time.

Task uncertainty is caused when employees cannot predict the inputs, processes, or outputs of their work (Griffin, Neal, and Parker, 2007; Cordery et al., 2010). There is also a relationship between the complexity of a task and the uncertainty of a task, although it is unclear in which direction causality flows (Campbell, 1988).

The effects of task uncertainty are less broad ranging than the effects of role uncertainty, but it does lead to lower performance (Griffin, Neal, and Parker, 2007; Cooper et al., 2015). An important element of that lower performance is that task uncertainty—and specifically *switching between tasks*—increases the length of time required to complete the tasks.

While distinct, the three types of uncertainty are all related to each other. The relationship is especially strong between job uncertainty and role uncertainty (Ashford, Lee, and Bobko, 1989; Dahl, 2011). For all three types of uncertainty, a key mediator between the uncertainty and its negative effects is externality of control (Nelson, Cooper, and Jackson, 1995; DiFonzo and Bordia, 1998). When employees feel like they no longer exert any personal control over their jobs, roles, and tasks, they feel helpless and become less motivated and less productive.[1]

---

[1] Some authors did not find links between various types of uncertainty and poor performance (Ashford, Lee, and Bobko, 1989; Schweiger and DeNisi, 1991). Indeed, Yun, Takeuchi, and Liu, 2007, found that for highly motivated employees, role ambiguity can increase parts of job performance as striving employees use role ambiguity as an excuse to try to impress management. However, another explanation is that performance is simply very

The literature identifies several steps that can be taken by managers to reduce uncertainty or ameliorate its negative effects. First, managers can reduce the frequency of organizational change (Rafferty and Griffin, 2006).[2] Importantly, it is not just the severity of change, but how often it occurs, that creates uncertainty. Indeed, in a qualitative examination of businesses, Charan and Colvin, 1999, found that effective CEOs launch relatively few major initiatives and make sure to launch new ones only when past changes have become "embedded in the company's DNA." Second, managers can carefully and openly plan for organizational change (DiFonzo and Bordia, 1998; Rafferty and Griffin, 2006). Employees who feel like there is a plan in place are less likely to panic when change does occur. Third, managers can improve communication with their employees about organizational changes and the roles of employees (Schweiger and DeNisi, 1991; DiFonzo and Bordia, 1998; Clampitt, DeKoch, and Cashman, 2000; Van Sell, Brief, and Schuler, 1981). However, one scholar argues that one-way communication, though vital, is not enough, and instead contends that employees must also be allowed to communicate their thoughts and concerns to management (Bordia et al., 2004).

Fourth, managers can work to create a culture of trust among staff and between staff and management (DiFonzo and Bordia, 1998).

Fifth, management can provide expert advisers to employees (Keith, Demirkan, and Goul, 2017). Keith, Demirkan, and Goul actually found that a positive effect of uncertainty is that it increases the willingness of employees to seek advice, which is associated with higher productivity.

Sixth, managers can involve employees in decisionmaking, which serves to empower them (Wall, Cordery, and Clegg, 2002; Prendergast, 2002; Cordery et al., 2010; Leifer and Mills, 1996). Indeed, empowering staff was a key recommendation in a recent RAND study on agile acquisition (Drezner and Simpson, 2017). In the literature on business science and management, decentralization, delegation, and empowerment have long been buzz words. However, these practices do not work for all business environments; they only improve employee productivity in uncertain workplaces in which close managerial supervision makes less sense. To go even further toward decentralization, managers can implement incentive-based pay structures in which employees are paid based on their outputs (Prendergast, 2002; Schiemann, 1987). This

---

hard to measure properly. Kull, 1978, defines productivity for most federal government employees as "output per staff year," which is difficult to quantify for most positions. Van Sell, Brief, and Schuler, 1981, further note that most studies on uncertainty have distressingly bad data collection methodology, relying upon self-reported values to measure performance. It is not so difficult to imagine that employees shy away from telling interviewers that their personal performance has worsened.

[2]   For the JRC in particular, reducing organizational change should be beneficial because frequent change has hampered the ability of contractors to work with the government (U.S. House of Representatives Committee on Armed Services, 2012).

gives employees the maximum amount of freedom to deal with uncertain tasks and increases employee motivation.

Centralized vs. Decentralized Decisionmaking

We find little academic literature specifically addressing how to get centralized decisions implemented by subunits. Most research occurs from the perspective of businesses deciding between implementing centralized or decentralized decisionmaking procedures, not from the perspective of government agencies trying to successfully implement already-existing centralized decisionmaking structures. Acemoglu et al., 2007, found that decentralization is preferable when there is an information imbalance, that is, when constituent parts have better information than central management. Similarly, Graham, Harvey, and Puri, 2015, found that CEOs specifically are more likely to delegate when they have less personal knowledge and greater need for information. Both these findings support the literature's recommendation that uncertainty can be mitigated by delegation.

Of most relevance is an older RAND report which investigated the problems of centralized control in the context of budgeting in DoD (Schlesinger, 1968). Schlesinger's work examined the 1961 "Revolution" in the Pentagon, during which the Office of the Secretary of Defense wrested more control over budgeting from the individual services. Schlesinger found that the Office of the Secretary of Defense was able to exert more control by (1) assuming budgetary powers; (2) setting budgets on a long-term time frame so that services tried to best use the money they had instead of fighting over next year's budget; and (3) giving the services a means to influence policy. Furthermore, "[a]ny organization must motivate subordinate levels by providing an opportunity to influence policy. In the absence of such exchanges, the chances for eliciting the necessary cooperation and support are slight" (Schlesinger, 1968). Schlesinger noted that the tendency over time is toward greater centralization but cautions that while the benefits of centralization are immediate and apparent, the costs that it imposes are less apparent but build up over time.

Understaffing

The literature on staffing treats it as a continuum between understaffed and overstaffed.[3] When a group has fewer members than needed to accomplish the minimum number of tasks, known as the maintenance minimum, in normal working hours, it is considered understaffed. Conversely, when a group has more members than it has capacity to deal with—for example, if a team had more members than desks available—then it is considered overstaffed.

---

[3]   Older research on understaffing refers to it as "undermanning."

The literature details many potential benefits from understaffing. Understaffing can boost motivation and creativity in teams (Weiss and Hoegl, 2016), increase willingness to listen to diverse viewpoints (Arnold and Greenberg, 1980), make members feel more involved (Wicker et al., 1976), increase team effectiveness (Campion, Papper, and Medsker, 1996), and lower costs, through both lower payroll and lower costs of coordination in smaller teams (Kessler, 2000). In teams that are understaffed, team members feel the need to band together and work harder to make up for their smaller numbers.

Much of the early research on understaffing suggests that the relationship between performance and staffing levels is curvilinear, with the apex at slightly understaffed (Vecchio and Sussmann, 1981). However, the benefits of understaffing should not be overstated.

First, the literature is not united; some authors find that understaffed groups are less productive (Ganster and Dwyer, 1995) and that understaffing can hurt profits in retail environments (Mani, Kesavan, and Swaminathan, 2015).

Second, while the literature lacks a consensus about the short-term effects of understaffing, there is widespread agreement that chronic understaffing leads to uniformly negative consequences (Weiss and Hoegl, 2016). Chronic understaffing leads to stress, burnout, depression, reduced motivation, and lower performance (Hudson and Shen, 2015; Ganster and Rosen, 2013). This makes intuitive sense: If a team member is unexpectedly sick, a team might come together and work harder to pick up the slack. However, this type of increased effort is not sustainable in the long-term.

Hudson and Shen, 2015, break understaffing down into three dimensions: the manpower dimension of understaffing, which simply measures by how much a group is understaffed; the type of personnel understaffing, which is whether a group lacks needed expertise; and the length of understaffing, which is whether understaffing is acute or chronic. Chronic understaffing is almost always negative, and those negative effects are magnified when groups lack necessary experts.

Understaffing is also of interest to the JRC for its effect on conformance quality. Conformance quality is how well employees carry out central management directives and standard operating procedures. It is often defined in contrast to service quality, which is the extent to which customers rate their service experience positively. Conformance quality increases productivity, timeliness, cost, business performance, and life-cycle productivity (Maani, Putterill, and Sluti, 1994; White, 1996; Krishnan et al., 2000).

In a longitudinal analysis of 268 stores of a large retailer, one scholar found that increasing staffing levels increased conformance quality (Ton, 2008). With a higher staffing level, workers felt less pressure to run around addressing immediate concerns and had more time to devote to fulfilling central management directives, like properly displaying merchandise and carrying out inventory checks. Indeed, other scholars show that lower staffing levels lead workers to cut corners when performing tasks

(Oliva and Sternman, 2001). Crucially, this corner cutting is not always immediately apparent to managers, who often believe that increased effort, not lower conformance, from their employees is what caused the higher productivity. This finding calls into doubt the earlier research on the benefits of understaffing.

Control Loss and Optimal Organization Size

Related to understaffing is the literature on control loss. Control loss is the dilution of control that central management has over the components of an organization. The primary finding from this literature is that when organizations increase in size, there is a tradeoff between increasing the number of employees and decreasing management's control over them (Williamson, 1967). In effect, organizations are like a game of telephone, with each additional layer of hierarchy increasing the chance that central management's message will be muddied. In general, organizations that have less time to make decisions and that employ higher-quality individuals as decisionmakers tend to have smaller optimal sizes (Gradstein, Nitzan, and Paroush, 1990). Regardless of the number of levels of hierarchy, control loss, much like uncertainty, can be reduced through effective communication and trust (Narayanaswamy, Grover, and Henry, 2013).

Effects of Certification

The literature on the effects of certification focus mainly on organizational certifications, especially certifications from the International Organization for Standardization (ISO). Many scholars have found benefits to ISO 9000, ISO 14000, and ISO 20000 certifications, which govern business management, environmental practices, and information technology management, respectively (Gotzamani and Tsiotras, 2001; Kuo et al., 2009; Rondinellia and Vastagb, 2000; Morrow and Rondinelli, 2002; Sharma, 2005; Cots, Casadesus, and Marimon, 2016). However, some scholars have found mixed results or negative results (Chow-Chua, Goh, and Wan, 2003; Link and Naveh, 2006; Terziovski, Samson, and Dow, 1997).

Fewer studies have been done on the effects of individual certification, but they have had similarly mixed results. One study found that a particular certification, the Project Management Professional Development Programme, improved knowledge of core management practices (Alam et al., 2008). However, two scholars have called into question the effectiveness of the widely used Project Management Professional (PMP) certification. After eliciting from experts 15 core competencies for potential information technology (IT) project managers, they surveyed over 3,000 IT managers and executives to determine which competencies were important. PMP certification was deemed the least important, with only 15.4 percent of responders considering it important (Stevenson and Starkweather, 2010). In a follow-up study, the same authors showed that the success rates for PMP certified employees versus non-certified employees were statistically indistinguishable. Moreover, interviews with IT executives provided anecdotal evidence that certification did not improve effectiveness, with one executive stating, "PMP is basically worthless. There is no correlation between a good project manager and certification based on my 15 years of experience" (Starkweather and Stevenson, 2011).

The effectiveness of certifications for other professions also has mixed scholarly endorsement. One certification program for nurses improved perceptions of empowerment while state certification programs for teachers improved wages but had no effect on teacher quality (Piazza et al., 2006; Angrist and Guryan, 2008). For acquisitions more specifically, one study from within the Defense Acquisition University found that high-level acquisitions classes did increase knowledge of the acquisition process, but it is unclear whether that finding can be generalized to certification programs in general (Court, Prothero, and Wood, 2015). In short, the literature on certification programs lacks consensus on their effectiveness.

Interview Methodology

Interviews supporting the discussion in Chapter Four were collected using the following protocols. Each interview was conducted by two RAND researchers with one or two JRC staff members. Interviews were conducted primarily in person with a minority conducted telephonically to meet staff availability needs. Interviews occurred in late November 2017 at the JRC office at the main facility in the DHS Nebraska Avenue Complex. All but two interviews occurred in person. We interviewed the entire JRC staff and leadership that was available, 12 individuals. JRC leadership—defined as the director and director of analysis—received the Executive Interview protocol. JRC analysts—defined as those with the Program Analyst job description—received the Analysis protocol, and all other staff members received the PMO protocol based on internal JRC organizational divisions. Once complete researcher interview notes were compared for consistency, and findings were reported if presented by over three-fourths of relevant interview subjects (three out of four analysts, nine out of 12 overall interview subjects, etc.).

Business Processes Study—Executive Interviews

We are conducting a study on behalf of the JRC to review its business practices, and recommend actions to improve efficiency, effectiveness, and plans for the future. Today's discussion will help us gain perspective on the key missions and objectives of the JRC, and the role it plays in supporting DHS missions and goals.

1. What is your role in the JRC? How long have you been in your position at the JRC?
   a. What aspects of the JRC do you provide leadership for?
2. What are the key mission objectives of the JRC?
   a. What are the key things that the JRC does to achieve its goals?
3. How, in your view, does JRC contribute to broader DHS missions and goals?
4. As we understand it a large part of the JRIMS process is working with components and sponsors. What types of activities do you do in coordination with these entities?

    a.   How does this coordination impact the JRIMS process?

    b.   Aside from components and sponsors, are there any other key entities you coordinate with? If so who?

5.   How do you think the JRC will change in the foreseeable future?

    a.   How will this affect your workflow or the workflow of your staff?

    b.   Are any related changes or planning efforts presently underway?

Business Processes Study—Analysis Interviews

We are conducting a study on behalf of the JRC to review its business practices, and recommend actions to improve efficiency, effectiveness, and plans for the future. As part of this study, today's discussion will help us gain perspective from people in your position at the JRC on the tasks you work on, what is required to complete those tasks, and any challenges you might experience in your work.

1.   What is your role in the JRC? How long have you been in your position at the JRC?

2.   We understand that most [of] your workload is dedicated to the JRIMS process. To better understand your role in this process, we'll be asking about the steps involved in, and any challenges you may face, working JRIMS.

    a.   What percentage of your time do you spend on JRIMS activities?

    b.   What aspects of JRIMS are you involved in?

    c.   What materials/documents/etc. do you use to complete these steps?

    d.   Do you coordinate with other JRC employees to complete this work? If so who, how, and how often?

    e.   On what types of activities do you coordinate with components and sponsors? Who do you coordinate with, how and how often?

    f.   What, if any, challenges are there with completing the JRIMS process?

       i. How often do these challenges occur?

       ii. What, in your opinion are the sources of these challenges?

3.   While JRIMS is a large part of your job, we understand that other activities may also be part of your workload. What are some of these activities you spend time on outside of the JRIMS process?

    a.   Who internal to JRC do you coordinate with to complete these activities? External to JRC?

    b.   How much time do you spend on these activities?

    c.   Are there any challenges to completing these other activities?

    d.   How do these activities impact your work on the JRIMS process?

4.   What would you say are the most predictable aspects of your job? What would you say are the most unpredictable?

Business Processes Study—Program Management Office Interviews

We are conducting a study on behalf of the JRC to review its business practices, and recommend actions to improve efficiency, effectiveness, and plans for the future. As part of this study, today's discussion will help us gain perspective from people in your position at the JRC on the tasks you work on, what is required to complete those tasks, and any challenges you might experience in your work.

1. What is your role in the JRC? How long have you been in your position at the JRC?
2. We understand that most [of] your workload is dedicated to program management. To better understand your role in this process, we'll be asking about the steps involved in, and any challenges you may face, working in the JRC.
    a. What program management activities are you involved in?
    b. What percentage of your time do you spend on these activities?
    c. What materials/documents/etc. do you use to complete these steps?
    d. Do you coordinate with other JRC employees to complete this work? If so who, how, and how often?
    e. On what types of activities do you coordinate with components and sponsors? Who do you coordinate with, how and how often?
    f. What, if any, challenges are there with completing these activities?
        i.   How often do these challenges occur?
        ii. What, in your opinion are the sources of these challenges?
    g. Aside from components and sponsors, are there any other key entities you coordinate with? If so who?
3. While program management is a large part of your job, we understand that other activities may also be part of your workload. What are some of these activities you spend time on outside of program management?
    a. Who internal to JRC do you coordinate with to complete these activities? External to JRC?
    b. How much time do you spend on these activities?
        i.   Are there any challenges to completing these other activities?
4. What would you say are the most predictable aspects of your job? What would you say are the most unpredictable?

Relevant RAND Reports

Butler, Dwayne M., Anthony Atler, Stephen M. Worman, Lily Geyer, and Bonnie Magnuson-Skeels, *Identifying Efficiencies in the Supply Chain for Training Ammunition: Methods, Models, and Recommendations*, Santa Monica, Calif.: RAND Corporation, RR-952-A, 2016. As of May 21, 2018:
https://www.rand.org/pubs/research_reports/RR952.html

Cook, Cynthia R., Emma Westerman, Megan McKernan, Badreddine Ahtchi, Gordon T. Lee, Jenny Oberholtzer, Douglas Shontz, and Jerry M. Sollinger, *Contestability Frameworks: An International Horizon Scan*, Santa Monica, Calif.: RAND Corporation, RR-1372-AUS, 2016. As of May 21, 2018:
https://www.rand.org/pubs/research_reports/RR1372.html

Drezner, Jeffrey A., Parisa Roshan, and Thomas Whitmore, *Enhancing Management of the Joint Future Vertical Lift Initiative*, Santa Monica, Calif.: RAND Corporation, RR-2010-OSD/JS, 2017. As of May 21, 2018:
https://www.rand.org/pubs/research_reports/RR2010.html

Drezner, Jeffrey A., and Michael Simpson, *Exploring Parallel Development in the Context of Agile Acquisition: Analytical Support to the Air Superiority 2030 Enterprise Capability Collaboration Team*, Santa Monica, Calif.: RAND Corporation, RR-1808-AF, 2017. As of May 21, 2018:
https://www.rand.org/pubs/research_reports/RR1808.html

Kavanagh, Jennifer, Megan McKernan, Kathryn Connor, Abby Doll, Jeffrey A. Drezner, Kristy N. Kamarck, Katherine Pfrommer, Mark V. Arena, Irv Blickstein, William Shelton, and Jerry M. Sollinger, *Joint Precision Approach and Landing System Nunn-McCurdy Breach Root Cause Analysis and Portfolio Assessment Metrics for DoD Weapons Systems*, Vol. 8, Santa Monica, Calif.: RAND Corporation, MG-1171/8-OSD, 2015. As of May 21, 2018:
https://www.rand.org/pubs/monographs/MG1171z8.html

Lewis, Leslie, John Schrader, William L. Schwabe, and Roger A. Brown, *Joint Warfighting Capabilities (JWCA) Integration: Report on Phase 1 Research*, Santa Monica, Calif.: RAND Corporation, MR-872-JS, 1998. As of May 21, 2018:
https://www.rand.org/pubs/monograph_reports/MR872.html

Loredo, Elvira N., John E. Peters, Karlyn D. Stanley, Matthew E. Boyer, William Welser IV, and Thomas S. Szayna, *Authorities and Options for Funding USSOCOM Operations*, Santa Monica, Calif.: RAND Corporation, RR-360-SOCOM, 2014. As of May 21, 2018:
https://www.rand.org/pubs/research_reports/RR360.html

McKernan, Megan, Nancy Y. Moore, Kathryn Connor, Mary E. Chenoweth, Jeffrey A. Drezner, James Dryden, Clifford A. Grammich, Judith D. Mele, Walter Nelson, Rebeca Orrie, Douglas Shontz, and Anita Szafran, *Issues with Access to Acquisition Data and Information in the Department of Defense: Doing Data Right in Weapon System Acquisition*, Santa Monica, Calif.: RAND Corporation, RR-1534-OSD, 2017. As of May 21, 2018:
https://www.rand.org/pubs/research_reports/RR1534.html

Paul, Christopher, Isaac R. Porche III, and Elliot Axelband, *The Other Quiet Professionals: Lessons for Future Cyber Forces from the Evolution of Special Forces*, Santa Monica, Calif.: RAND Corporation, RR-780-A, 2014. As of May 21, 2018:
https://www.rand.org/pubs/research_reports/RR780.html

Schlesinger, James R., *Defense Planning and Budgeting: The Issue of Centralized Control*, Santa Monica, Calif.: RAND Corporation, P-3813, 1968. As of May 21, 2018:
https://www.rand.org/pubs/papers/P3813.html

References

Acemoglu, Daron, Philippe Aghion, Claire Lelarge, John Van Reenen, and Fabrizio Zilibott, "Technology, Information, and the Decentralization of the Firm," *Quarterly Journal of Economics*, Vol. 122, No. 4, 2007, pp. 1759–1799.

Alam, Mehmood, Andrew Gale, Mike Brown, and Callum Kidd, "The Development and Delivery of an Industry Led Project Management Professional Development Programme: A Case Study in Project Management Education and Success Management," *International Journal of Project Management*, Vol. 26, No. 3, 2008, pp. 223–237.

Allison, George, "The Venator-110, Could This Be Britain's Future Light Frigate?" *UK Defence Journal*, September 15, 2016. As of November 28, 2017:
https://ukdefencejournal.org.uk/venator-110-britains-future-light-frigate/

Anderson, Jonathan R., "Managing Employees in the Service Sector: A Literature Review and Conceptual Development," *Journal of Business and Psychology*, Vol 20, No. 4, 2006, pp. 501–523.

Angrist, Joshua D., and Jonathan Guryan, "Does Teacher Testing Raise Teacher Quality? Evidence from State Certification Requirements," *Economics of Education Review*, Vol. 27, No. 5, 2008, pp. 483–503.

Arnold, David W., and Carl I. Greenberg, "Deviate Rejection Within Differentially Manned Groups," *Social Psychology Quarterly*, Vol. 43, No. 4, 1980, pp. 419–424.

Ashford, Susan J., Cynthia Lee, and Philip Bobko, "Content, Causes, and Consequences of Job Insecurity: A Theory-Based Measure and Substantive Test," *Academy of Management Journal*, Vol. 32, No. 4, 1989, pp. 803–829.

Australian Department of Defence, "Capability, Acquisition, and Sustainment Group: Home," webpage, undated. As of November 28, 2017:
http://www.defence.gov.au/casg/

———, "2016 Defence White Paper," 2016. As of November 28, 2017:
http://www.defence.gov.au/whitepaper/Docs/2016-Defence-White-Paper.pdf

Australian National Audit Office, "2015–2016 Major Projects Report: Department of Defence," February 28, 2017. As of November 28, 2017:
https://www.anao.gov.au/sites/g/files/net4181/f/ANAO_Report_2016-2017_40a.pdf

Bordia, Prashant, Elizabeth Hobman, Elizabeth Jones, Cindy Gallois, and Victor J. Callan, "Uncertainty During Organizational Change: Types, Consequences, and Management Strategies," *Journal of Business and Psychological*, Vol. 18, No. 4, 2004, pp. 507–532.

Brissett, Wilson, "The School of JROC," *Air Force Magazine*, March 2017, pp. 54–58.

Brown, Bryan D., "U.S. Special Operations Command: Meeting the Challenges of the 21st Century," *Joint Forces Quarterly*, Vol. 40, 2006, pp. 38–43.

Campbell, Donald J., "Task Complexity: A Review and Analysis," *Academy of Management Review*, Vol. 13, No. 1, 1988, pp. 40–52.

Campion, Michael A., Ellen M. Papper, and Gina J. Medsker, "Relations Between Work Team Characteristics and Effectiveness: A Replication and Extension," *Personnel Psychology*, Vol. 49, No. 2, 1996, pp. 429–452.

Canadian Armed Forces, "Terms of Reference for the Independent Review Panel for Defence Acquisition," webpage, July 7, 2016. As of November 28, 2017: http://www.forces.gc.ca/en/business-how-to-do/irpda-terms-of-reference.page

Caplan, Robert D., and Kenneth W. Jones, "Effects of Work Load, Role Ambiguity, and Type A Personality on Anxiety, Depression, and Heart Rate," *Journal of Applied Psychology*, Vol. 60, No. 6, 1975, pp. 713–719.

Chairman of the Joint Chiefs of Staff, Joint Capabilities Integration and Development System, Washington, D.C.: Director, Joint Staff, Instruction 3170.01 I, January 23, 2015.

Charan, Ram, and Geoffrey Colvin, "Why CEOs Fail," *Forbes*, 1999.

Chow-Chua, Clare, Mark Goh, and Tan Boon Wan, "Does ISO 9000 Certification Improve Business Performance?" *International Journal of Quality and Reliability Management*, Vol. 20, No. 8, 2003, pp. 936–953.

Clampitt, Phillip G., Robert J. DeKoch, and Thomas Cashman, "A Strategy for Communicating About Uncertainty," *Academy of Management Executive*, Vol. 14, No. 4, 2000, pp. 41–57.

Cook, Stephen, Stan Nowakowski, and Mark Unewisse, "A System-of-Systems Engineering Approach for Australian Land Force Capability Integration," *Defence Science and Technology Organization*, September 2012.

Cooper, Patrick S., Paul M. Garrett, Jaime L. Rennie, and Frini Karayanidis, "Task Uncertainty Can Account for Mixing and Switch Costs in Task-Switching," *PLOS One*, Vol. 10, No. 6, 2015, pp. 1–17.

Cordery, John L., David Morrison, Brett M. Wright, and Toby D. Wall, "The Impact of Autonomy and Task Uncertainty on Team Performance: A Longitudinal Field Study," *Journal of Organizational Behavior*, Vol. 31, No. 2–3, 2010, pp. 240–258.

Cots, Santi, Marti Casadesus, and Frederic Marimon, "Benefits of ISO 20000 IT Service Management Certification," *Information Systems and E-Business Management*, Vol. 14, No. 1, 2016, pp. 1–18.

Court, Charles M., Gregory B. Prothero, and Roy L. Wood, "The Value of Training: Analysis of DAU's Requirements Management Training," *Defense Acquisition Research Journal*, Vol. 22, No. 2, 2015, pp. 155–173.

Dahl, Michael S., "Organizational Change and Employee Stress," *Management Science*, Vol. 57, No. 2, 2011, pp. 240–256.

Defense Acquisition University, *Introduction to Defense Acquisition Management*, 6th ed., Fort Belvoir, Va.: Defense Acquisition University Press, 2003.

———, "DOTmLPF-P Analysis," last modified May 21, 2018. As of July 9, 2018: https://www.dau.mil/acquipedia/Pages/ArticleDetails. aspx?aid=d11b6afa-a16e-43cc-b3bb-ff8c9eb3e6f2

DHS—*See* U.S. Department of Homeland Security.

DiFonzo, Nicholas, and Prashant Bordia, "A Tale of Two Corporations: Managing Uncertainty During Organizational Change," *Human Resource Management*, Vol. 37, No. 3–4, 1998, pp. 295–303.

DoD—*See* U.S. Department of Defense.

Evans, Peter B., "Multiple Hierarchies and Organizational Control," *Administrative Science Quarterly*, Vol. 20, No. 2, 1975, pp. 250–259.

Freedberg, Sydney J. Jr., "JROC Speeds Up and Opens Up: Reforming the Dark Heart of Acquisition," *Breaking Defense*, April 19, 2016. As of November 28, 2017:
https://breakingdefense.com/2016/04/
jroc-speeds-up-opens-up-reforming-the-dark-heart-of-acquisition/

Gans, Noah, Ger Koole, and Avishai Mandelbaum, "Telephone Call Centers: Tutorial, Review, and Research Prospects," *Manufacturing and Service Operations Management*, Vol. 5, No. 2, 2003, pp. 79–141.

Ganster, Daniel C., and Deborah J. Dwyer, "The Effects of Understaffing on Individual and Group Performance in Professional and Trade Occupations," *Journal of Management*, Vol. 21, No. 2, 1995, pp. 175-190.

Ganster, Daniel C., and Christopher C. Rosen, "Work Stress and Employee Health: A Multidisciplinary Review," *Journal of Management*, Vol. 39, No. 5, 2013, pp. 1085–1122.

GAO—*See* U.S. Government Accountability Office.

Gotzamani, Kateria D., and George D. Tsiotras, "An Empirical Sutdy of the ISO 9000 Standards' Contribution Towards Total Quality Management," *International Journal of Operations and Production Management*, Vol. 21, No. 10, 2001, pp. 1326–1342.

Gradstein, Mark, Shmuel Nitzan, and Jacob Paroush, "Collective Decision-Making and the Limits on the Organization's Size," *Public Choice*, Vol. 66, No. 3, 1990, pp. 279–291.

Graham, John R., Campbell R. Harvey, and Manju Puri, "Capital Allocation and Delegation of Decision-Making Authority Within Firms," *Journal of Financial Economics*, Vol. 115, No. 3, 2015, pp. 449–470.

Griffin, Mark A., Andrew Neal, and Sharon K. Parker, "A New Model of Work Role Performance: Positive Behavior in Uncertain and Interdependent Contexts," *Academy of Management Journal*, Vol. 50, No. 2, 2007, pp. 327–347.

Harknett, Richard J., and James A. Stever, "The Struggle to Reform Intelligence After 9/11," *Public Administration Review*, Vol. 71, No. 5, 2011, pp. 700–706.

Hudson, Cristina K., and Winny Shen, "Understaffing: An Under-Researched Phenomenon," *Organizational Psychology Review*, Vol. 5, No. 3, 2015, pp. 244–263.

Independent Review Panel for Defence Acquisition, "2015–2016 Annual Report," 2016. As of November 28, 2017:
http://www.forces.gc.ca/assets/FORCES_Internet/docs/en/business-how-to-do/
irpda-2015-2016-annual-report-.pdf

IRPDA—*See* Independent Review Panel for Defence Acquisition.

Jackson, Susan E., and Randall S. Schuler, "A Meta-Analysis and Conceptual Critique of Research on Role Ambiguity and Role Conflict in Work Settings," *Organization Behavior and Human Decision Processes*, Vol. 36, No. 1, 1985, pp. 16–78.

Keith, Mark, Haluk Demirkan, and Michael Goul, "The Role of Task Uncertainty in IT Project Team Advice Networks," *Decision Sciences*, Vol. 48, No. 2, 2017, pp. 207–247.

Kerzner, Harold, *Project Management: A Systems Approach to Planning, Scheduling and Controlling*, 8th ed., Florence, Ky.: John Wiley and Sons, 2003.

Kessler, Eric H., "Tightening the Belt: Methods for Reducing Development Costs Associated with New Product Innovation," *Journal of Engineering and Technology Management*, Vol. 17, No. 1, 2000, pp. 59–92.

Krishnan, M. S., C. H. Kriebel, Sunder Kekre, and Tridas Mukhopadhyay, "An Empirical Analysis of Productivity and Quality in Software Products," *Journal of Management Science*, Vol. 46, No. 6, 2000, pp. 745–759.

Kull, Donald C., "Productivity Programs in the Federal Government," *Public Administration Review*, Vol. 38, No. 1, 1978, pp. 5–9.

Kuo, Tsuang, Tsun-Jin Chang, Kuei-chung Hung, and Ming-yuan Lin, "Employees' Perspective on the Effectiveness of ISO 9000 Certification: A Total Quality Management Framework," *Total Quality Management and Business Excellence*, Vol. 20, No. 12, 2009, pp. 1321–1335.

Leifer, Richard, and Peter K. Mills, "An Information Processing Approach for Deciding Upon Control Strategies and Reducing Control Loss in Emerging Organizations," *Journal of Management*, Vol. 22, No. 1, 1996, pp. 113–137.

Link, Sharon, and Eitan Naveh, "Standardization and Discretion: Does the Environmental Standard ISO 14001 Lead to Performance Benefits?" *IEEE Transactions on Engineering Management*, Vol. 53, No. 4, 2006, pp. 508–519.

Locher, James R. III, "Has It Worked? The Goldwater-Nichols Reorganization Act—Department of Defense Reorganization," U.S. Naval War College, article adapted from address delivered May 8, 2001. As of November 28, 2017:
http://users.clas.ufl.edu/zselden/Course%20Readings/Locher.pdf

Lowenthal, Mark M., *Intelligence: From Secrets to Policy*, Los Angeles, Calif.: CQ Press, 2016.

Maani, K. E., M. S. Putterill, and D. G. Sluti, "Empirical Analysis of Quality Improvement in Manufacturing," *International Journal of Quality and Reliability Management*, Vol. 11, No. 7, 1994, pp. 19–37.

Macgregor, Douglas A., "A Decade, No Progress," *Joint Forces Quarterly*, Vol. 25, 2000, pp. 18–23.

Machina, Fran, "Resourcing Special Operations," briefing slides, presented to the American Society of Military Comptrollers, May 30, 2014. As of November 28, 2017:
http://www.asmconline.org/wp-content/uploads/2014/06/30-Machina.pdf

Mani, Vidya, Saravanan Kesavan, and Jayashankar M. Swaminathan, "Estimating the Impact of Understaffing on Sales and Profitability in Retail Stores," *Productions and Operations Management*, Vol. 24, No. 2, 2015, pp. 201–218.

McConnell, Mike, "Overhauling Intelligence," *Foreign Affairs*, Vol. 86, No. 4, 2007, pp. 49–58.

Meinhart, Richard M., "Vice Chairmen of the Joint Chiefs of Staff and Leadership of the Joint Requirements Oversight Council," *Joint Forces Quarterly*, Vol. 56, 2010, pp. 144–151.

Morrow, David, and Dennis Rondinelli, "Adopting Corporate Environmental Management Systems: Motivations and Results of ISO 14001 and EMAS Certification," *European Management Journal*, Vol. 20, No. 2, 2002, pp. 159–171.

Moyle, Penny, and Katharine Parkes, "The Effects of Transition Stress: A Relocation Study," *Journal of Organizational Behavior*, Vol. 20, No. 5, 1999, pp. 625–646.

Narayanaswamy, Ravi, Varun Grover, and Raymond M. Henry, "The Impact of Influence Tactics in Information System Development Projects: A Control-Loss Perspective," *Journal of Management Information Systems*, Vol. 30, No. 1, 2013, pp. 191–225.

Nelson, Adrian, Cary L. Cooper, and Paul R. Jackson, "Uncertainty Amidst Change: The Impact of Privatization on Employee Job Satisfaction and Well-Being," *Journal of Occupational and Organizational Psychology*, Vol. 68, 1995, pp. 57–71.

New Zealand Defence Force, "Capital Equipment Acquisition—What We Do," web page, January 8, 2013. As of November 28, 2017:
http://www.nzdf.mil.nz/what-we-do/capital-equip-acquisition.htm

New Zealand Defence Force and New Zealand Ministry of Defence, "Briefing for the Incoming Minister of Defence," October 2014. As of November 28, 2017:
http://www.nzdf.mil.nz/downloads/pdf/public-docs/2014/election-brief-october-2014.pdf

———, "The 2014–2015 Annual Report," 2015. As of November 28, 2017:
http://www.nzdf.mil.nz/downloads/pdf/public-docs/nzdf-annual-report-2015.pdf

New Zealand Ministry of Defence, "Defence Capability Plan 2016," 2016a. As of November 28, 2017:
http://www.nzdf.mil.nz/downloads/pdf/public-docs/2016/defence-capability-plan-2016.pdf

———, "Defence White Paper 2016," 2016b. As of November 28, 2017:
http://www.nzdf.mil.nz/downloads/pdf/public-docs/2016/defence-white-paper-2016.pdf

Office of the Director of National Intelligence, "Joint Intelligence Community Council Meets," Washington, D.C., June 25, 2007.

———, "U.S. National Intelligence: An Overview," 2011. As of November 28, 2017:
https://www.hsdl.org/?view&did=697740

Oliva, Rogelio, and John D. Sterman, "Cutting Corners and Working Overtime: Quality Erosion in the Service Industry," *Management Science*, Vol. 47, No. 7, 2001, pp. 894–914.

Omand, Sir David, "Creating Intelligence Communities," *Public Policy and Administration*, Vol. 25, No. 1, 2010, pp. 99–116.

Owens, William A., "The American Revolution in Military Affairs," *Joint Forces Quarterly*, Vol. 10, 1996, pp. 37–38.

———, "JROC: Harnessing the Revolution in Military Affairs," *Joint Forces Quarterly*, Vol. 5, 1994, pp. 55–57.

Packard, David, *Quest for Excellence: Final Report to the President*, Washington, D.C.: Government Printing Office, 1986.

Perry, David, "2015 Status Report on Major Defence Equipment Procurements," policy paper, *Centre for Military and Strategic Studies, University of Calgary*, December 2015.

Piazza, Irene M., Moreen Donahue, Patricia C. Dykes, Mary Quinn Griffin, and Joyce J. Fitzpatrick, "Differences in Perceptions of Empowerment Among Nationally Certified and Noncertified Nurses," *Journal of Nursing Administration*, Vol. 36, No. 5, 2006, pp. 277–283.

Pollard, Tessa M., "Changes in Mental Well-Being, Blood Pressure and Total Cholesterol Levels During Workplace Reorganization: The Impact of Uncertainty," *Work and Stress*, Vol. 15, No. 1, 2001, pp. 14–28.

Prendergast, Canice, "The Tenuous Trade-off Between Risk and Incentives," *Journal of Political Economy*, Vol. 110, No. 5, 2002, pp. 1071–1102.

Priest, Dana, and William M. Arkin, "'Top Secret America': A Look at the Military's Joint Special Operations Command," *Washington Post*, September 2, 2011. As of November 28, 2017:
https://www.washingtonpost.com/world/national-security/
top-secret-america-a-look-at-the-militarys-joint-special-operations-command/2011/08/30/
gIQAvYuAxJ_story.html?utm_term=.423a8df877c2

Public Law 108-458, Intelligence Reform and Terrorism Prevention Act of 2004, Section 1031, Joint Intelligence Community Council, December 27, 2004.

Public Law 110-417, Duncan Hunter National Defense Authorization Act for Fiscal Year 2009, Section 3001, October 14, 2008.

Public Law 111-23, Weapon Systems Acquisition Reform Act of 2009, May 22, 2009.

Pugliese, David, "Conservative Government Appoint Defence Procurement Panel," *Ottawa Citizen*, June 1, 2015. As of January 31, 2018:
http://ottawacitizen.com/news/national/defence-watch/
conservative-government-appoints-defence-procurement-panel

Rafferty, Alannah E., and Mark A. Griffin, "Perceptions of Organizational Change: A Stress and Coping Perspective," *Journal of Applied Psychology*, Vol. 91, No. 5, 2006, pp. 1154–1162.

Rizzo, John R., Robert J. House, and Sidney I. Lirtzman, "Role Conflict and Ambiguity in Complex Organizations," *Administrative Science Quarterly*, Vol. 15, No. 2, 1970, pp. 150–163.

Roman, Peter J., and David W. Tarr, "The Joint Chiefs of Staff: From Service Parochialism to Jointness," *Political Science Quarterly*, Vol. 113, No. 1, 1998, pp. 91–111.

Rondinellia, Dennis, and Gyula Vastagb, "Panacea, Common Sense, or Just a Label? The Value of ISO 14001 Environment Management Systems," *European Management Journal*, Vol. 18, No 5, 2000, pp. 499–510.

Sargut, Gökçe, and Rita McGrath, "Learning to Live with Complexity," *Harvard Business Review*, September 2011.

Schiemann, William A., "The Impact of Corporate Compensation and Benefit Policy on Employee Attitudes and Behavior and Corporate Profitability," *Journal of Business and Psychology*, Vol. 2, No. 1, 1987, pp. 8–26.

Schmidt, Susanne, Ulrike Roesler, Talin Kusserow, and Renate Rau, "Uncertainty in the Workplace: Examining Role Ambiguity and Role Conflict, and Their Link to Depression—A Meta-Analysis," *European Journal of Work and Organizational Psychology*, Vol. 23, No. 1, 2014, pp. 91–106.

Schuler, Randall S., "Role Conflict and Ambiguity as a Function of Task-Structure-Technology Interaction," *Organizational Behavior and Human Performance*, Vol. 20, 1977, pp. 66–74.

Schwartz, Moshe, *Defense Acquisitions: How DOD Acquires Weapon Systems and Recent Efforts to Reform the Process*, Washington, D.C.: Congressional Research Service, April 23, 2010. As of November 27, 2017:
http://www.dtic.mil/get-tr-doc/pdf?AD=ADA520832

Schweiger, David M., and Angelo S. DeNisi, "Communication with Employees Following a Merger: A Longitudinal Field Experiment," *The Academy of Management Journal*, Vol. 34, No. 1, 1991, pp. 110–135.

Sharma, Divesh S., "The Association Between ISO 9000 Certification and Financial Performance," *The International Journal of Accounting*, Vol. 40, No. 2, 2005, pp. 151–172.

Siegel, Donald S., and Kenneth Simons, "Assessing the Effects of Mergers and Acquisitions on Firm Performance, Plant Productivity, and Workers: New Evidence from Matched Employer-Employee Data," *Strategic Management Journal*, Vol. 31, No. 8, 2010, pp. 903–916.

Sloan, Elinor, "Canadian Defence Commitments: Overview and Status of Selected Acquisitions and Initiatives," *University of Calgary, The School of Public Policy, SPP Research Papers*, Vol. 6, No. 36, 2013.

———, "Something Has to Give: Why Delays Are the New Reality of Canada's Defence Procurement Strategy," *Centre for Military and Strategic Studies, University of Calgary*, October 2014.

Starkweather, Jo Ann, and Deborah H. Stevenson, "PMP Certification as a Core Competency: Necessary but Not Sufficient," *Project Management Journal*, Vol. 42, No. 1, 2011, pp. 31–41.

Stevenson, Deborah H., and Jo Ann Starkweather, "PM Critical Competency Index: IT Execs Prefer Soft Skills," *International Journal of Project Management*, Vol. 28, No. 7, 2010, pp. 663–671.

Stewart, Jenny, and Tony Ablong, "When Australian Defence Procurement Goes Wrong: Improving Outcomes in a Troubled Contractual Environment," *Economic and Labour Relations Review*, Vol. 24, No. 2, 2013, pp. 238–254.

Stone, J. C., "A Separate Defence Procurement Agency: Will It Actually Make a Difference?" Canadian Defence and Foreign Affairs Institute, Strategic Studies Working Group, February 2012.

Tang, Yung-Tai, and Chen-Hua Chang, "Impact of Role Ambiguity and Role Conflict on Employee Creativity," *African Journal of Business Management*, Vol. 4, No. 6, 2010, pp. 869–881.

Terziovski, Mile, Danny Samson, and Douglas Dow, "The Business Value of Quality Management Systems Certification. Evidence from Australia and New Zealand," *Journal of Operations Management*, Vol. 15, No. 1, 1997, pp. 1–18.

Ton, Zeynep, "The Effect of Labor on Profitability: The Role of Quality," Harvard Business School working paper, 2008.

United Kingdom Ministry of Defence, "Terms of Reference for the Defence Audit Committee," March 2013. As of November 28, 2017:
https://www.gov.uk/government/uploads/system/uploads/attachment_data/file/224069/20130204_mar13_dac_tors.pdf

———, "How Defence Works," Version 4.2, December 1, 2015. As of November 28, 2017:
https://www.gov.uk/government/uploads/system/uploads/attachment_data/file/484941/20151208HowDefenceWorksV4_2.pdf

United Kingdom Parliament, "Decision-Making in Defence Policy: Government Response to the Committee's Eleventh Report of Session 2014–2015," webpage, July 21, 2015. As of November 28, 2017:
https://publications.parliament.uk/pa/cm201516/cmselect/cmdfence/367/36704.htm

U.S. Code, Title 10, Section 181, Joint Requirements Oversight Council, December 23, 2016.

———, Section 2366a, Major Defense Acquisition Programs: Determination Required Before Milestone A Approval, December 23, 2016.

———, Section 2366b, Major Defense Acquisition Programs: Certification Required Before Milestone B Approval, December 23, 2016.

———, Section 2433, Unit Cost Reports, January 7, 2011.

———, Section 2433a, Critical Cost Growth in Major Defense Acquisition Programs, January 2, 2013.

———, Section 2448a, Program Cost, Fielding, and Performance Goals in Planning Major Defense Acquisition Programs, December 23, 2016.

U.S. Code, Title 50, Section 3022, Joint Intelligence Community Council, December 17, 2004.

U.S. Department of Defense Instruction 5000.02, Operation of the Defense Acquisition System, Washington, D.C.: Under Secretary of Defense for Acquisition, Technology, and Logistics, January 7, 2015.

U.S. Department of Homeland Security, Charter of DHS Joint Requirements Council, Management Directive 1405, September 17, 2003.

———, Department of Homeland Security Manual for the Operation of the Joint Requirements Integration and Management System, Instruction Manual 107-01-001-01, April 21, 2016.

U.S. Government Accountability Office, Results Oriented Cultures: Implementation Steps to Assist Mergers and Organizational Transformations, Washington, D.C., GAO-03-669, July 2003.

———, High Risk Series: An Update, Washington, D.C., GAO-09-271, January 2009a.

———, Defense Acquisitions: Charting a Course for Lasting Reform, Washington, D.C., Testimony Before the Committee on Armed Services, House of Representatives, April 30, 2009b.

———, Defense Management: Perspectives on the Involvement of the Combatant Commands in the Development of Joint Requirements, Washington, D.C., GAO-11-527R, May 2011.

———, Defense Management: Guidance and Progress Measures Are Needed to Realize Benefits from Changes in DOD's Joint Requirements Process, Washington, D.C., GAO-12-339, February 2012.

———, Homeland Security Acquisitions: Joint Requirements Council's Initial Approach Is Generally Sound and It Is Developing a Process to Inform Investment Priorities, Washington, D.C., GAO-17-171, October 2016.

———, High Risk Series: Progress on Many High-Risk Areas, While Substantial Efforts Needed on Others, Washington, D.C., GAO-17-317, February 2017.

U.S. House of Representatives, Implementing Management for Performance and Related Reforms to Obtain Value in Every Acquisition Act, Bill 5013, 2010.

U.S. House of Representatives Committee on Armed Services, "Challenges to Doing Business with the Department of Defense: Findings of the Panel on Business Challenges in the Defense Industry," March 19, 2012.

U.S. Joint Chiefs of Staff, "J8: Force Structure, Resource and Assessment," webpage, undated. As of November 28, 2017:
http://www.jcs.mil/Directorates/J8-Force-Structure-Resources-Assessment/

U.S. Office of Management and Budget, Preparation, Submission and Execution of the Budget, Office of Management and Budget Circular A-11, Washington, D.C., 2015.

Van Sell, Mary, Arthur P. Brief, and Randall S. Schuler, "Role Conflict and Role Ambiguity: Integration of the Literature and Directions for Future Research," Human Relations, Vol. 34, No. 1, 1981, pp. 43–71.

Vecchio, Robert P., and Mario Sussmann, "Staffing Sufficiency and Job Enrichment: Support for an Optimal Level Theory," Journal of Occupational Behaviour, Vol. 2, 1981, pp. 177–187.

Wall, Toby D., John L. Cordery, and Chris W. Clegg, "Empowerment, Performance, and Operational Uncertainty: A Theoretical Integration," Applied Psychology: An International Review, Vol. 51, No. 1, 2002, pp. 146–169.

Weiss, Matthias, and Martin Hoegl, "Effects of Relative Team Size on Teams with Innovative Tasks: An Understaffing Theory Perspective," *Organizational Psychology Review*, Vol. 6, No. 4, 2016, pp. 324–351.

White, Gregory P., "A Meta-Analysis Model of Manufacturing Capabilities," *Journal of Operations Management*, Vol. 14, 1996, pp. 315–331.

Wicker, Allan W., "Undermanning Theory and Research: Implications for the Study of Psychological and Behavioral Effects of Excess Human Populations," *Representative Research in Social Psychology*, Vol. 4, No. 1, 1973, pp. 185–206.

Wicker, Allan W., Sandra L. Kirmeyer, Lois Hanson, and Alexander Dean, "Effects of Manning Levels on Subjective Experiences, Performance, and Verbal Interaction in Groups," *Organizational Behavior and Human Performance*, Vol. 17, No. 2, 1976, pp. 251–274.

Williamson, Oliver E., "Hierarchical Control and Optimum Firm Size," *Journal of Political Economy*, Vol. 75, No. 2, 1967, pp. 123–138.

Yun, Seokhwa, Riki Takeuchi, and Wei Liu, "Employee Self-Enhancement Motives and Job Performance Behaviors: Investigating the Moderating Effects of Employee Role Ambiguity and Managerial Perceptions of Employee Commitment," *Journal of Applied Psychology*, Vol. 92, No. 3, 2007, pp. 745–756.